MONDAY — Patterning and Algebra

1. Find the value of **x**.

   $x + 23 = 55$

2. Find the value of **t**.

   $3 \times 8 = t + 15$

3. What is the pattern rule?

   2, 5, 11, 23, 47, 95

4. What will be the 8th term of this pattern?

   400, 385, 370, 355, 340

5. Write the first three numbers of this pattern rule.

   start at 3, multiply by 2

   _____, _____, _____

TUESDAY — Number Sense

1. If there are 25 apples in each basket, how many apples are in 11 baskets?

2. Order these numbers from least to greatest.

   28 989, 28 229, 28 998

3. Find the product:

   125 x 0.1

4. Write this number in words.

   234 340

5. If 3 novels cost $21.75, how much is one novel?

WEDNESDAY Geometry

1. Draw a parallelogram.

2. What kind of triangle is this?

   A. scalene   B. right   C. equilateral

3. Flip this shape

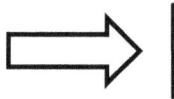

4. How many lines of symmetry are there in a rectangle?

5. Is this an acute, obtuse or right angle?

THURSDAY Measurement

1. 3 km = _____ cm

2. 700 mm = _____ km

3. What unit of measure would you use to measure the height of a building?

   A. km   B. m   C. cm

4. Find the area of a rectangle with the dimensions of 8 m by 7 m.

5. Find the perimeter of this rectangle.

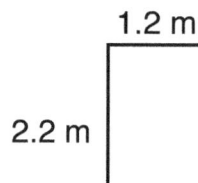

   1.2 m

   2.2 m

FRIDAY Data Management

Martin loved to read the sports section of the newspaper on the weekend because it gave an updated list of the local high school teams standings. Here are this week's standings in basketball:

Team	Points Scored
Panthers	68
Pumas	62
Tigers	59
Giraffes	50
Ravens	50
Mustangs	28
Stingrays	26

Use the information in the table to answer the following questions.

1. What is the range of the data? _____

2. What team is leading in points scored? _____

3. What is the mean of the data? _____

4. What is the mode? _____

5. What is the best kind of graph to display this data? _____

BRAIN STRETCH

Identify each number as either **prime (P)** or **composite (C)**.

1. 68 _____

2. 87 _____

3. 9 _____

4. 23 _____

5. 44 _____

6. 100 _____

MONDAY — Patterning and Algebra

1. Show the first three numbers of this pattern.

   start at 3, multiply by 10

   _____, _____, _____

2. $888 \div 8 =$

3. Complete the pattern.

   25, 125, 225, 325, _____, 525

4. Create a growing pattern.

5. What will be the 9th figure in this pattern?

   ⬠ ◯ ◇ ⬠

TUESDAY — Number Sense

1. List these numbers in order from least to greatest.

   19 912, 9129, 9291

2. Write $876.90 in words.

3. Choose >, <, or =.

   2.24 ☐ 2.42

4. Order these fractions from least to greatest.

   $\frac{4}{8}$ $\frac{7}{8}$ $\frac{1}{8}$ $\frac{5}{8}$

5.

   $50\overline{)4050}$

WEDNESDAY Geometry

1. How many faces does a triangular prism have?

2. What is an angle of 90° called?

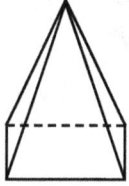

   A. obtuse   B. right   C. acute

3. Name this shape.

4. How many vertices does an octagon have?

5. Draw an obtuse angle.

THURSDAY Measurement

1. Hannah trims her hair every four months. If she last cut it in May, in what month should she schedule her next haircut?

2. Which would take longer, crossing the street or baking a cake?

3. 5 L=_____ ml

4. How many decades in 130 years?

5. Compare the following using: > , < or =

   2 months [   ] 65 days

Data Management

Mr. McLean's math class measured the height of each student.
Here are the results:

Larry 125 cm	Susan 140 cm
Martin 156 cm	Monique 129 cm
Neesha 148 cm	Naomi 132 cm
Sam 141 cm	Baxter 159 cm
Lashia 138 cm	Liam 160 cm
Stuart 155 cm	Cameron 161 cm
Camille 129 cm	Ethan 142 cm
Nathaniel 142 cm	Corrine 158 cm
Kate 135 cm	Shamila 142 cm
Nancy 129 cm	Daniel 140 cm

Use the data listed to answer these questions:

1. How many students are in the sample? _____

2. What is the range of the data?_____

3. What is the mode?_____

4. Who is the tallest? _____

BRAIN STRETCH

David and his 2 brothers were given $30 each. How much money do they have altogether?

MONDAY — Patterning and Algebra

1. 100 ÷ 10 = _____

2. 300 - 199 = _____

3. Complete the pattern.

   99, 88, 77, 66, ____, ____, 33

4. Write the first three numbers of this pattern:

   start at 3, multiply by 5

   ____, ____, ____

5. Fill in the blank to make the equation true.

   25 x _____ = 200 - 125

TUESDAY — Number Sense

1. Ten packs of gum cost $12.90. How much is one pack?

2. What fraction is shaded?

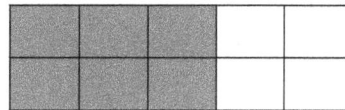

3. 34.2 x 10

4. Order these numbers from greatest to least.

   1001, 1101, 1011, 1110

5. Round 1299 to the nearest 10.

WEDNESDAY Geometry

1. What is the name of this shape?

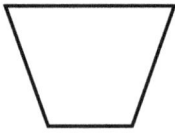

2. How many lines of symmetry does this letter have?

U

3. Are these shapes congruent or similar?

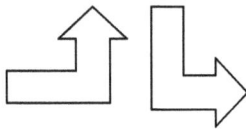

4. A rhombus is a polygon with how many sides?

5. Draw an acute angle.

THURSDAY Measurement

1. 40 weeks =____months

2. 690 dm =_____m

3. What is the area of a square with 2 cm sides?

4. How many days in 2 years?

5. A can of soda usually has:

   A. 1000 ml

   B. 355 ml

   C. 10 ml

Data Management

Georgina surveyed her classmates and friends to see what kind of movies they liked to watch for her media literacy class. Here are her results:

Comedy	Horror	Drama	Animation
卌 卌 卌 卌 Ⅲ	卌 卌 Ⅲ	卌 卌 Ⅲ	卌 卌 卌 卌

1. What is the most popular type of movie? _____

2. What is the least popular type of movie? _____

3. What is the range of the data? _____

4. How many people did she survey? _____

5. What could her survey question have been?

_____

BRAIN STRETCH

State the place value of the underlined digit in each number:

1. 31<u>4</u> 098 _____

2. 31 4<u>5</u>8 _____

3. <u>9</u>0 738 _____

4. 961 27<u>3</u> _____

5. 5<u>7</u>6 239 _____

6. <u>2</u>16 892 _____

1. Extend the pattern.

    500, 496, 492, ____, ____, ____

2. What are the first three numbers of this pattern?

    start at 30, add 8

    ____, ____, ____

3. What is the pattern rule of this pattern?

    3, 12, 48, 192, 768

4. What should replace the ____ to make the following equation true?

    ____ + 34 = 50 - 2

5. Complete the equivalent fraction.

    $\dfrac{3}{8} = \dfrac{}{24}$

TUESDAY Number Sense

1. Round 5633 to the nearest hundred.

2. Write all of the factors for 14.

3. What number comes just after 1126?

4. Draw the money needed to represent $14.98 using the fewest number of coins and bills.

5. Choose >, <, or =.

    120.3 ☐ 120.3

WEDNESDAY — Geometry

1. What 3D figure does this object look like?

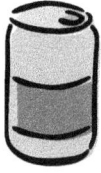

   A. cube   B. sphere   C. cylinder

2. Look at the shapes. Choose flip, slide or turn.

   A. flip   B. slide   C. turn

3. What 3D shape can you make with this net?

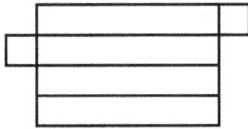

4. What is the name of this shape?

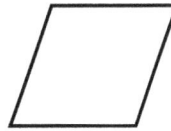

5. What is a quadrilateral?

THURSDAY — Measurement

1. 8.9 ml = _____ cl

2. The time is 10:43 pm. What time will it be in 21 minutes?

3. Which has a greater volume, a kitchen garbage can or a can of soda pop?

4. Find the perimeter of the trapezoid.

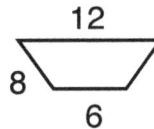

   12
   8
   6

5. Complete the following using >,< or =:

   1 century [ ] 97 years

Data Management

Megan and Kaitlyn are playing with a six sided number cube.

1. How many possible outcomes are there? _____

2. What is one of the possible outcomes? _____

3. What is the probability of rolling an odd number? _____

4. What is the probability of rolling an even number? _____

5. What is the probability of rolling a six? _____

BRAIN STRETCH

How many squares can you find below?

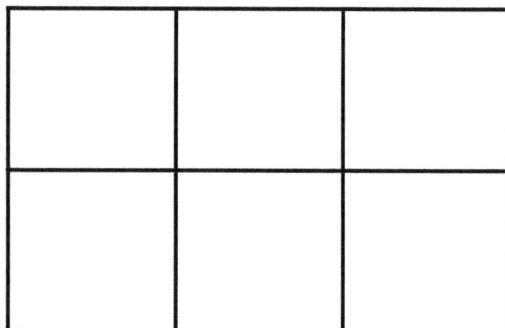

© Chalkboard Publishing

MONDAY — Patterning and Algebra

1. Create a repeating pattern.

2. Fill in the blank to make the equation true.

$$36 \div 6 = 2 \times \underline{\hspace{1cm}}$$

3. What is the pattern rule?

37, 33, 29, 25, 21, 17

4. Fill in the missing numbers:

7, 12, 17, _____, _____, 32

5. What kind of pattern is this?

99, 88, 77, 66, 55, 44

A. repeating   B. growing   C. shrinking

TUESDAY — Number Sense

1. What fraction is not shaded?

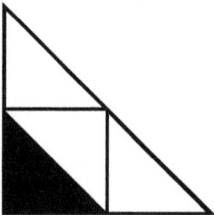

2. Order these numbers from least to greatest.

782, 872, 702, 827

3. How many eggs in 5 dozen?

A.   60 eggs

B.   72 eggs

C.   56 eggs

4. Write the numeral for:

nine thousand four hundred and seventy-one

5. Write $77.35 in words.

WEDNESDAY Geometry

1. What is the name of this 3D figure?

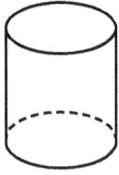

2. What shape is the face of a cylinder?

3. How many vertices does a triangle have?

4. Classify the angle.

   A. acute B. straight C. right

5. How many lines of symmetry does this shape have?

THURSDAY Measurement

1. What measuring tool would you use to measure the length of a summer holiday?

   A. calendar   B. scale   C. ruler

2. What is the perimeter of a square that has 2.4 mm sides?

3. How many weeks in 6 years?

4. What is the best estimate of the mass of Sara's eyeglasses?

   A. 100 g
   B. 100 mg
   C. 100 kg

5. 12 m = _____ mm

FRIDAY — Data Management

Answer these questions with one of the following possibilities:

impossible   unlikely   likely   certain

1. How likely is it to snow this winter? _____

2. How likely is it to rain this summer?   _____

3. How likely are you to brush your teeth today? _____

4. How likely are you to use the telephone today? _____

5. How likely are you to read a book today? _____

6. How likely are you to watch T.V. today? _____

BRAIN STRETCH

1.	2.	3.	4.	5.
53	72	6.1	3.7	8.4
x 45	x 63	x 3.2	x 2.2	x 8.5

MONDAY — Patterning and Algebra

1. ____ - 67 = 21

2. Create a growing pattern.

3. Complete the pattern:

   6, 12, 24, 48, ____, ____

4. Fill in the blank to make this equation true.

   $66 - 40 = 13 \times$ ____

5. What is the pattern rule?

   50, 49, 47, 44, 40, 35, 29

TUESDAY — Number Sense

1. List all the factors for 40.

2. Draw the money needed to represent this amount, using the fewest number of bills and coins.

   $50.23

3. Order these fractions from least to greatest:

   5/9, 2/9, 7/9

4. $693.1 \div 100 =$

5. Write 8954 in words.

WEDNESDAY   Geometry

1. How many lines of symmetry does this letter have?

   D

2. Is this a net for a cube?

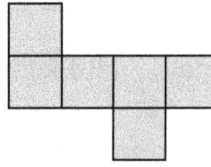

3. What is this 3D figure called?

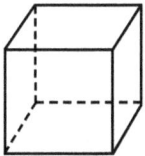

5. How many edges does a cube have?

4. Is a 34 degree angle obtuse, acute or right?

THURSDAY   Measurement

1. What measurement tool would you use to find the length of a music lesson?

   A. clock   B. scale   C. calendar

2. What is the year 1 decade after 1978?

3. What is the perimeter of this irregular polygon?

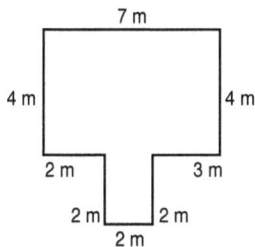

   7 m

   4 m   4 m

   2 m   3 m

   2 m   2 m

   2 m

4. 22 cm = ___ mm

5. How long might it take to comb your hair?

   A. 1 hour   B. 1 minute   C. 1 day

FRIDAY Data Management

Match the math term with its definition.

A. Probability   B. Mean   C. Data   D. Graph   E. Bar Graph

F. Median   G. Range   H. Pictograph   I. Mode   J. Circle Graph

1. _____ found by dividing the sum of the numbers by the number of numbers in the set.

2. _____ the middle number in a set of numbers arranged in order.

3. _____ the value that occurs most often in a set of data.

4. _____ a visual representation of data.

5. _____ a graph in which a circle is used to display data.

6. _____ a graph that uses pictures to display data.

7. _____ facts or information.

8. _____ a number from zero to one that shows how likely it is that an event will happen.

9. _____ a graph made up of horizontal or vertical bars.

10. _____ the difference between the smallest value and the greatest value in set of data.

BRAIN STRETCH

Write these numbers in expanded form.

1. 132 547 _____

2. 33 651 _____

3. 94 830 _____

4. 191 234 _____

       Week 6

MONDAY — Patterning and Algebra

1. Fill in the missing number:

   121, 123, 125, _____, 129, 131

2. What is the pattern rule?

   1, 11, 21, 31, 41, 51

3. 1001 - 54 = _____

4. Write the first three numbers in this pattern:

   start at 72, add 8

5. 346 = 700 - _____

TUESDAY — Number Sense

1. Write as a numeral:

   six hundred fifty-five thousand twelve

2. $3\overline{)3699}$

3. Round 1982 to the nearest ten.

4.
   3477
   - 2913

5. Mr. Davis has 31 students and 80 pieces of pizza. Each student is going to have the same amount to eat. How many pieces can each student have?

© Chalkboard Publishing

WEDNESDAY Geometry

1. What is the name of this 3D figure?

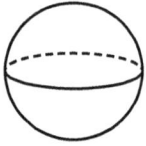

2. How many faces does a square based pyramid have?

3. Look at the shapes. Choose flip, slide or turn.

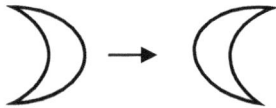

A. flip   B. slide   C. turn

4. How many sides does a rhombus have?

5. Classify the following pair of lines.

A. intersecting   B. parallel   C. perpendicular

THURSDAY Measurement

1. Michael watches 1hr and 30 minutes of TV before bedtime. If he goes to bed at 9 pm, when does he start to watch TV? How many hours does he watch in a week?

2. What is the perimeter of a heptagon with 9 m sides?

3. What is the answer in grams?

3642 g + 67 mg + 6879 g =

4. Megan can type 31 words per minute. How many words can she type in 2 hours?

5. 6820 g =_____kg

Here is the number of students in grades 4, 5, and 6 at Clara Breton Public School.

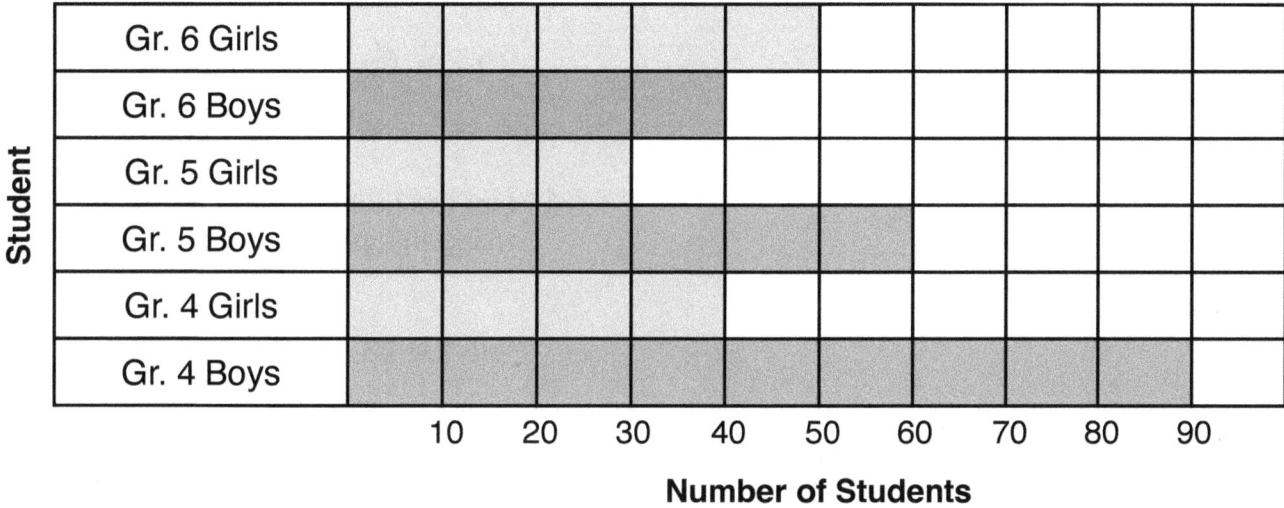

Student											
Gr. 6 Girls											
Gr. 6 Boys											
Gr. 5 Girls											
Gr. 5 Boys											
Gr. 4 Girls											
Gr. 4 Boys											
	10	20	30	40	50	60	70	80	90		

Number of Students

1. How many students are there in grades 4, 5, and 6 altogether?_____

2. How many boys are there? _____

3. How many girls are there? _____

4. What type of graph is this? _____

5. Which grade has more girls than boys? _____

BRAIN STRETCH

Marianne spent 3 hours at swim practice each week.

1) How many hours a year does she practice swimming?

2) How many hours will she have practised in 10 years?

MONDAY — Patterning and Algebra

1. What will be the 11th number in this pattern?

   100, 96, 92, 88, 84

2. What should replace the _____ to make the following equation true?

   $9 + 2 = 66$ _____ 55

   A. +   B. -   C. ÷

3. $900 + b = 1012$

   $b =$ _____

4. List the first three numbers using this pattern rule.

   start at 23   x 2 - 10

5. What is the rule for the following pattern:

   500, 50, 5, 0.5, 0.05, 0.005

TUESDAY — Number Sense

1. Subtract:

   $789.50 - $12.99

2. What is the place value of the number in **bold?**

   58 **4**59

3. What is the difference between 9.4 and 3.7?

4. What is 482 937 in expanded form?

5. What is the greatest common factor of 18 and 72?

WEDNESDAY Geometry

1. What is the name of this 3D figure?

2. Which of these shapes could never have perpendicular lines?

   A. circle   B. square   C. rectangle

3. Draw an obtuse angle.

4. Calculate the measure of the missing angle.

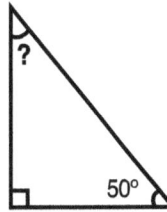

   50°

5. How many lines of symmetry does this letter have?

   G

THURSDAY Measurement

1. What is the perimeter of a heptagon with 8 m sides?

2. What would the temperature be if it were snowing?

   A. -2°C   B. 9°C   C.19°C

3. 55.9 cm = _____m

4. What unit of measurement would you use to find a person's body mass?

   A. kg   B. L   C. km

5. How many minutes are in 4 hours and 16 minutes?

Here is a circle graph that shows how students get to school. Use the information to answer the questions.

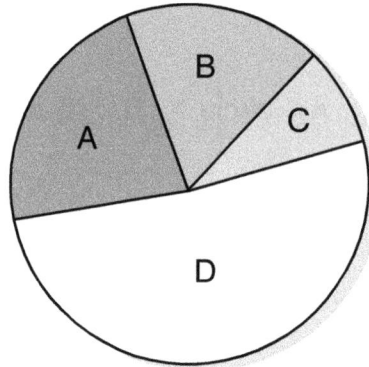

A - Drive 21%

B - Walk 18%

C - Bike 9%

D - Take the bus 52%

1. If the school has 90 students, how many students walk to school?

2. What fraction of the students drive to school?

3. What fraction of the students take the bus?

4. What percentage of students either walk or drive to school?

5. What is the most popular way to get to school?

BRAIN STRETCH

A bus travels at 80 km/hr.

1) How far will it go in 5 hours?

2) How far will it go in 10 hours?

MONDAY — Patterning and Algebra

1. Extend the following pattern:

   10, 19, 37, 73, ___, ___, ___

2. What is the rule for the following pattern?

   1, 4, 19, 94, 469, 2344

3. List the first three numbers in this pattern:

   start at 454, subtract 10

4. $96 + n = 123$

   $n =$ _____

5. Is this a growing, shrinking or repeating pattern?

   75, 100, 125, 150, 175

TUESDAY — Number Sense

1. Compare using: < > or =

   0.7 _____ 0.53

2. Add: $45.99 + $34.89

3. Write 128 400 in words.

4. Which number is prime?

   A. 908   B. 40   C. 11

5. Complete the equivalent fraction.

   $$\frac{7}{9} = \frac{}{72}$$

WEDNESDAY — Geometry

1. Why is a rectangle called a quadrilateral?

2. Calculate the measure of the missing angle.

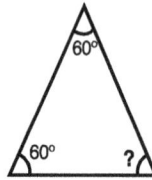

3. Draw a 90 degree angle.

4. What is the name of this 3D figure?

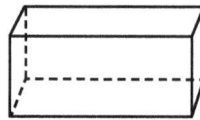

5. Which 3D figure doesn't have a curved surface?

   A. cylinder   B. cone   C. triangular prism

THURSDAY — Measurement

1. How many months in 7 years?

2. 37 cl = _____ ml

3. Calculate the area of this triangle.

4. 370 m = _____ km

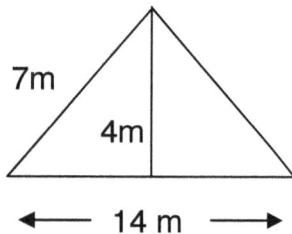

5. What unit of measurement would you use to find the height of a ferris wheel?

Data Management

Use the information from the pictograph to answer the questions.

Number of Books Read

Spencer	◇◇◇◇◇◇
Ben	◇◇◇◇◇◇◇
Madelyn	◇◇◇◇◇
Megan	◇◇◇◇◇◇
Michael	◇◇◇◇◇
Kaitlyn	◇◇◇◇◇◇◇◇

◇ = 4 books

1. How many books were read altogether? _____

2. Who read the most books? _____

3. Which two people read the same number of books? _____

4. How many books did Michael and Ben read together? _____

5. How many more books did Kaitlyn read than Spencer? _____

BRAIN STRETCH

What is the better buy? Show your work.

1. $300 for 20 books

2. $36 for 4 books

MONDAY   Patterning and Algebra

1. What is the rule for the following pattern:

   78, 778, 7778, 77778

2. What number is missing from the following sequence?

   18, 29, 40, 51, _____, 73

3. What will be the 8th number in this pattern?

   3, 30, 300, 3000, 30000

4. List the first three numbers for this pattern rule.

   start at 20, x 2 + 3

5. Simplify this expression using the order of operations.

   2 x 35 + 55 - 14

TUESDAY   Number Sense

1. Write 77.01 in expanded form.

2. Add:

   3.456 + 4.51

3. Write this fraction in its simplest form.

   $\frac{9}{12} =$

4. Multiply:

   527
   x 283

5. Change the mixed number to an improper fraction.

   $3 \frac{2}{5} =$

WEDNESDAY Geometry

1. Reflect this shape.

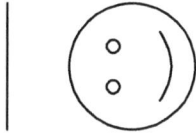

2. How many right angles can a triangle have?

3. If a triangle has a 20 degree angle and a 40 degree angle, what is the third angle?

4. How many lines of symmetry does this letter have?

H

5. How many vertices does a hexagon have?

THURSDAY Measurement

1. What unit of measurement would you use to find the width of your thumb?

2. What are the dimensions of a square with an area of $81m^2$?

3. How many years in a millennium?

4. How much time has elapsed in between 22:05:00 and 1:25:15?

5. What is the perimeter of this figure?

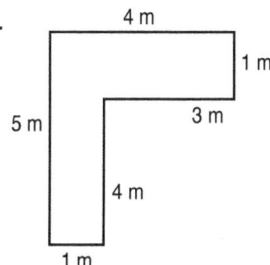

4 m

1 m

5 m

3 m

4 m

1 m

© Chalkboard Publishing

Here is a circle graph that shows students' favourite season. Use the information to answer the questions.

Students' Favourite Season

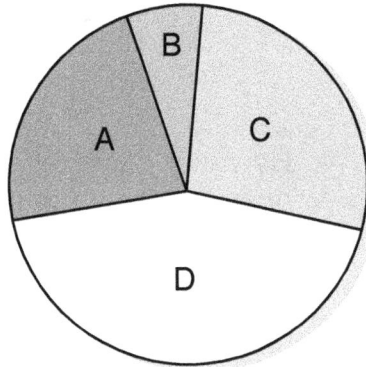

A - Spring   21%

B - Fall   9%

C - Winter   25%

D - Summer   45%

1. If the school has 80 students, how many students liked fall the best?

2. What fraction of the students liked winter?

3. What fraction of the students liked summer?

4. What percentage of students chose either spring or fall?

5. What is the most popular season?

BRAIN STRETCH

1. $22.7 \div 100 =$

2. $1.4 \div 100 =$

3. $86.5 \div 10 =$

4. $37.1 \div 10 =$

5. $572.2 \div 100 =$

6. $841.2 \div 100 =$

MONDAY — Patterning and Algebra

1. 100 x *n* = 1200

   n = ____

2. List the first three numbers using this pattern rule.

   start at 10, x3, - 15

3. What should replace the _____ to make the following equation true?

   6 x 11 = 100 _____ 34

   A. +   B. -   C. ÷

4. Is this a growing, shrinking or repeating pattern?

   102, 99, 96, 93, 90

5. Extend the following pattern:

   81, 72, 63, 54, _____, _____ , _____

TUESDAY — Number Sense

1. Subtract:

   45.669 - 4.390

2. Turn this improper fraction into a mixed number:

   $\frac{23}{4}$

3. Round this number to the nearest tenth.

   45 789.64

4. Which quotient is even?

   A. 49 ÷ 7   B. 80 ÷ 8   C. 18 ÷ 6

5. Multiply:

   745
   x 34

WEDNESDAY Geometry

1. Name a polygon that has less than 4 vertices.

2. Classify this angle as acute, obtuse, straight, or right.

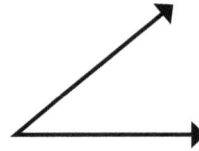

3. How many lines of symmetry does this letter have?

M

4. What do the interior angles of a triangle equal?

5. How many edges does a cone have?

THURSDAY Measurement

1. 2.99 dm = _____ mm

2. What is the area of the rectangle below?

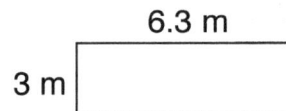

6.3 m

3 m

3. What unit of measurement would you use to find the mass of a bicycle?

4. How many decades are there in 40 years?

5. A rectangle has an area of 81 cm². The width is 9 cm. What is the length?

Data Management

Pop Tabs Collected

	Week 1	Week 2	Week 3
Monday	23	20	13
Tuesday	11	24	6
Wednesday	30	8	13
Thursday	18	17	28
Friday	11	15	8

1. What was the total number of pop tabs collected in week 1?

2. How many more pop tabs were collected on the Mondays than on the Tuesdays?

3. What was the mode of the number of pop tabs collected in week 3?

4. What was the mean of the number of pop tabs collected in Week 2?

BRAIN STRETCH

June has 30 days. It rained on 25 of those days.

1. What was the fraction of days in June that were rainy?

2. What was the percentage of days in June that were not rainy?

MONDAY — Patterning and Algebra

1. What will be the 7th number in this pattern?

   9000, 900, 90, 9, 0.9

2. $690 \div a = 6.9$

   $a =$ _____

3. Extend the following pattern:

   250, 235, 220, 205, _____, _____, _____

4. What should replace the _____ to make the following equation true?

   $16 + 64 = 8$ _____ 10

   A. x   B. ÷   C. -

5. Ben runs 8 km every day. How many km will Ben run in 25 days?

TUESDAY — Number Sense

1. How many dimes in 12 toonies?

2. Add:

   $$\frac{1}{2} + \frac{2}{6} =$$

3. What is the greatest possible number using the following digits?

   8 2 5 1 9

4. Write as a decimal:

   three tenths

5. Simplify the following expression using the proper order of operations.

   $71 + 41 - 3 \times 4$

WEDNESDAY   Geometry

1. What are the angles of an equilateral triangle?

2. What is an angle of 120° called?

   A. obtuse   B. right   C. acute

3. What 3D figure could be made from these pieces?

   A. cylinder

   B. rectangular prism

   C. pyramid

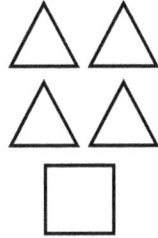

4. How many lines of symmetry does this letter have?

   Z

5. How many vertices does a rectangular prism have?

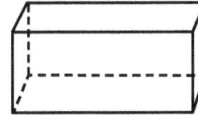

THURSDAY   Measurement

1. The time is 11:32 am. What time will it be in 85 minutes?

2. How many decades in 4 centuries?

3. Find the perimeter of the trapezoid.

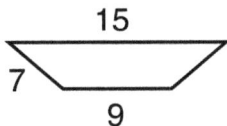

   15

   7

   9

4. Calculate the area of the parallelogram.

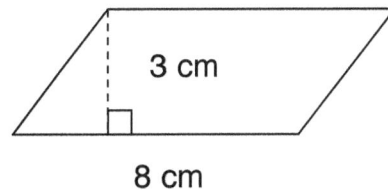

   3 cm

   8 cm

5. 73.1 km = _____ m

Data Management

Complete the chart.

Set of Data	Mean	Range	Median	Mode
1. 20, 11, 20, 12, and 18				
2. 3, 17, 6, 17, 19, and 16				
3. 23, 21, 21, 20, and 18				
4. 3, 2, 5, 5, and 5				
5. 10, 10, 25, 10, and 10				

BRAIN STRETCH

If an orange tree usually bears about 65 oranges, approximately how many orange trees must a farmer have to harvest 10 000 oranges?

MONDAY Patterning and Algebra

1. What will be the 19th shape in this pattern?

□ ◯ ▽ □

2. Is this a growing, shrinking or repeating pattern?

99, 88, 77, 99, 88, 77

3. Sherri gave away a quarter of her 1896 sticker collection. How many stickers does she have left?

4. Write the first three numbers for this pattern rule:

start at 10, double the number

5. $1.12 \times n = 11.2$

$n = \underline{\quad}$

TUESDAY Number Sense

1. Write the following as a fraction.

0.09

2. Write the following as a decimal.

$\dfrac{54}{100}$

3. Multiply: 34.5×8

4. Divide:

$16\overline{)1270}$

5. Simplify the following expression using the order of the operations.

$60 \div 4 + 18 \times 1 \times 20$

WEDNESDAY   Geometry

1. If a triangle has two angles that are 40 degrees, what kind of triangle is it?

2. How many lines of symmetry? does this letter have?

L

3. Find the volume of this box.

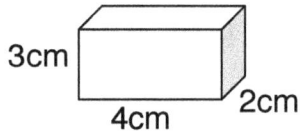

3cm
4cm
2cm

4. How many edges does this pyramid have?

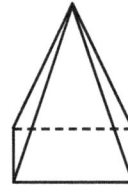

5. Look at the shapes. Name the transformation.

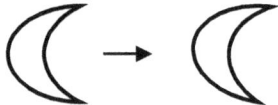

THURSDAY   Measurement

1. 18.5 dm = _____ cm

2. If a circle has a diameter of 6 cm, what is the radius?

3. Each side of a square measures 8 cm. What would the perimeter be if the sides were to increase by 3 cm?

4. What time is 15:00 on the 12 hour clock?

5. How many decades in 6 centuries?

Data Management

Here are the results of a Favourite Sports Survey. Football got 15 votes, baseball 25, basketball 20, and hockey 30.

1. Create a tally chart to show the information.

Football	Baseball	Basketball	Hockey

1. How many students voted altogether? _____

2. List the results from least to greatest.

   _____

3. How many students voted for either hockey or baseball?

4. What was the most popular sport? _____

5. What was the least popular sport? _____

BRAIN STRETCH

The cookie factory produces 4630 cookies a day. If the cookies are put in boxes of 24, how many boxes are needed? Round to the nearest whole number.

MONDAY — Patterning and Algebra

1. 77 - 11 = 3 x _____

2. 9 x _____ = 50 - 23

3. What number is missing from the following sequence?

    11, 22, 33, 44, _____, 66

4. What is the pattern rule?

    5, 8, 11, 14, 17, 20

5. Write the first three numbers for this pattern rule:

    start at 90, subtract 4

TUESDAY — Number Sense

1. How many eggs in 3 ½ dozen?

2. Order these numbers from least to greatest.

    1.01, 0.11, 1.10, 0.01

3. What is this expanded number in standard form?

    80 000 + 7000 + 400 + 80 + 1

4. What number is six thousand less than 129 904?

5. What is the lowest common multiple for 6 and 12?

WEDNESDAY · Geometry

1. Classify this angle.

2. How many lines of symmetry?

3. What 3D figure does this object look like?

4. Calculate the area of the parallelogram.

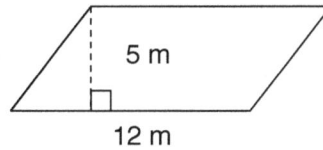

   5 m

   12 m

5. How many vertices does a quadrilateral have?

THURSDAY · Measurement

1. 6m = ___mm

2. What time is 20:00 on the 12 hour clock?

3. What is the area in square metres of a pool 14 m X 20 m?

4. What time is it?

   _____ : _____

5. Find the perimeter of regular pentagon that has 5 cm sides.

Data Management

Sort factors into the Venn Diagram, using the rules listed below.

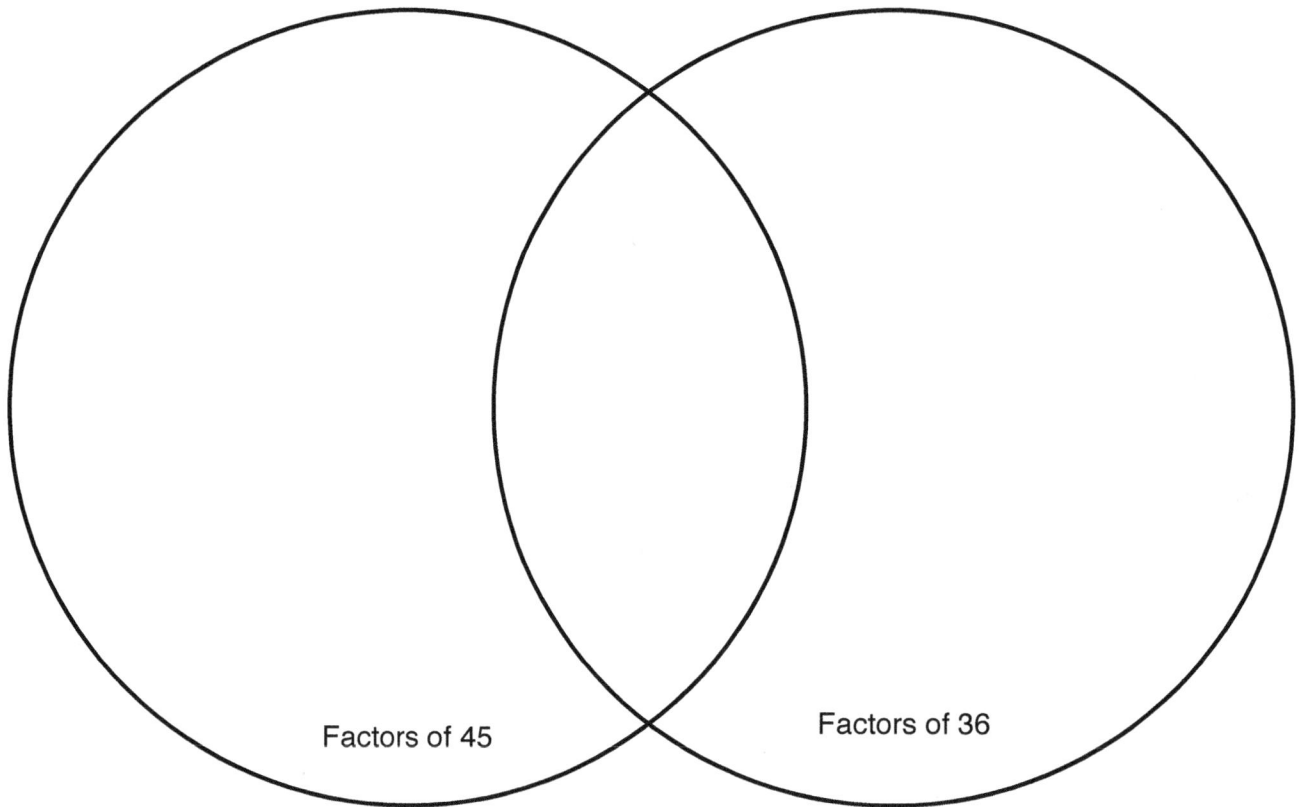

Factors of 45   Factors of 36

BRAIN STRETCH

A tin of Purrfect Cat Food is on sale for 25% off.

1) If its regular price is $3.20, what is the sale price?

2) How many cans can you buy for $5.00?

MONDAY — Patterning and Algebra

1. $7 \times n = 40 + 16$

   $n = \underline{\hspace{1cm}}$

2. Complete this table:

b	b X 8
1	
2	
3	
4	
5	

3. What is the pattern rule?

   30, 60, 90, 120, 150

4. Fill in the missing number.

   6, 24, 96, _____

5. What will be the 12th shape in this pattern?

TUESDAY — Number Sense

1. Subtract:

   $\begin{array}{r} 300.53 \\ - \ 199.30 \\ \hline \end{array}$

2. Which two numbers are both factors of 36?

   A. 9, 6   B. 6, 11   C. 4, 15

3. Ben is 25th in line. How many people are in front of him?

4. David ate 80 blueberries in an hour. How many did he eat in fifteen minutes?

5. Simplify the expression using the order of operations.

   $(8 + 1) \times (5 \times 5 - 1)$

WEDNESDAY — Geometry

1. Name a 3D figure that does _not_ have any edges.

2. How many lines of symmetry does this letter have?

X

3. Which figure shows a line of symmetry?

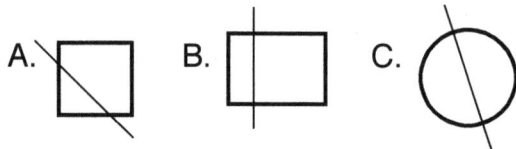

A. B. C.

4. What are the angles of an equilateral triangle?

5. Classify the following pair of lines.

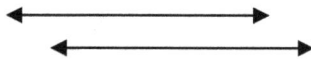

THURSDAY — Measurement

1. What unit of measure is best to measure the distance between two cities?

2. How many metres in 36 km?

3. What is the formula for the area of a triangle?

4. A rectangle has an area of 96 cm^2. The width is 12 cm. What is the length?

4. If a car is traveling 90km/hour, how far will it go in 2.5 hours?

Data Management

Tenzin's class surveyed his schoolmates to see what their favourite ice cream flavours were. Here are his results:

12 vanilla   **20 chocolate**   **6 strawberry**   **2 bubble gum**

Fill in this pictograph using the scale of 🍦 = 2 people.

Flavour	Number of People

1.   What is the range of the data?_____

2.   What is the mean?_____

3.   What is the most popular flavour?_____

4.   What is the least popular flavour?_____

BRAIN STRETCH

Sophie bought 3 T-shirts. Each T-shirt cost $22.50. How much did the T-shirts cost altogether? She paid with a $50 bill. Did she get change? Explain.

MONDAY Patterning and Algebra

1. Complete the following:

   395, 399, 403, 407,_____, _____, _____

2. 7 X _____ = 84

3. What will be the 18th shape in this pattern?:

4. Each spider has 8 legs. How many legs do 15 spiders have?

5. 45 ÷ ____ = 9

TUESDAY Number Sense

1. Name a prime number between 10 and 20.

2. Add: 489.12 + 0.999

3. Multiply:

$$\begin{array}{r} 0.06 \\ \times\ 0.02 \\ \hline \end{array}$$

4. Divide:

   22) 4444

5. List the integers in order from least to greatest.

   -11, 15, 9, -6, -10, 14

WEDNESDAY — Geometry

1. How are a square and a rectangle the same?

2. How many triangular faces does a tetrahedron have?

3. How many of the following pairs of lines intersect?

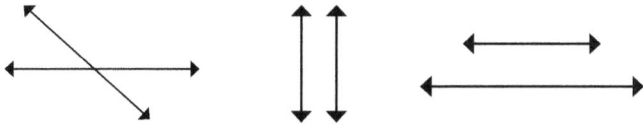

4. Classify the angle.

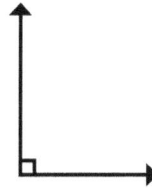

5. What is the size in degrees of the remaining angle if a triangle has angles of 60° and 90°?

THURSDAY — Measurement

1. 4000 m =_____ km

2. State the best unit measure to measure a drop of rain.

3. What time is 8:00 pm in 24 hour notation?

4. The time is 9:14 a.m.
   What time will it be in 79 minutes?

5. Find the perimeter of an octagon if all of the sides equal 9 m.

Data Management

Jordan is creating a board game to play with is brothers. He wants to design a spinner that is has these probabilities.

¼ green , ⅛ orange, ⅛ red, ⅜ blue, ⅛ purple

Please design a spinner for Jordan in the space below.

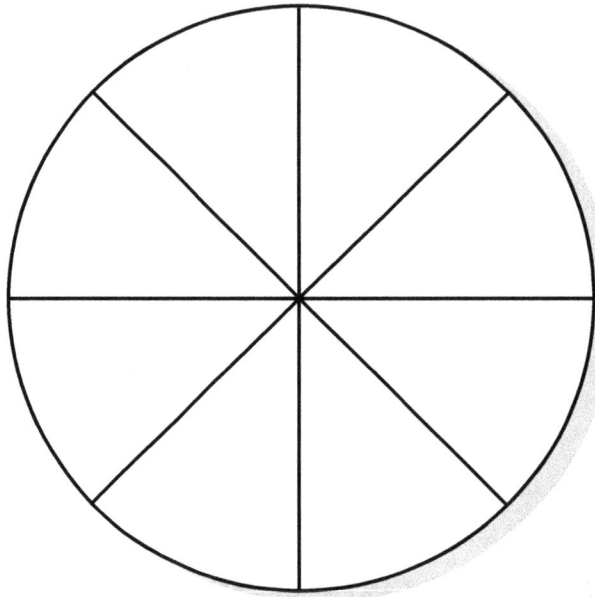

1. Which colour is the spinner most likely to land on? _____

2. Which colours have a 1/8 chance of being spun? _____

3. Which colour has the greatest chance of being spun? _____

4. Which colours have the least chance of being spun? _____

BRAIN STRETCH

If 72 chicken dinners cost $695, how much does 1 chicken dinner cost?
Round your answer to the nearest penny.

MONDAY — Patterning and Algebra

1. Divide: 78.8 by 4

2. Put the following numbers in order from least to greatest:

   5.22, 5.5, 5.6, 5.1

3. Multiply:

   $$\begin{array}{r} 0.598 \\ \times\ \ 4.200 \\ \hline \end{array}$$

4. Complete this table:

x	X + 14
1	
2	
3	
4	
5	

5. Simplify the expression using the order of operations.

   (973 - 465) - (5 + 53) + 394

TUESDAY — Number Sense

1. What is the next number if the pattern rule is "subtract 60"?

   120, _____

2. Fill in the missing number.

   999, 959, 919, _____

3. There were 234 people who attended a hockey game. If each ticket cost $11.00 how much money was collected?

4. What is the least possible number using the following digits?

   4 2 5 1 9

5. In which number sentence does a 4 make the equation true?

   A. 4 x _____ = 32   B. 16 ÷ _____ = 4   C. 24 + _____ = 30

WEDNESDAY — Geometry

1. How many lines of symmetry does a pentagon have?

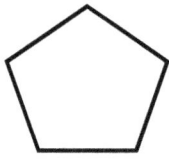

2. Which of these is an acute angle?

   A. 4°   B. 140°   C. 185°

3. Draw an obtuse angle.

4. Define a straight angle.

5. Which pair of shapes look congruent?

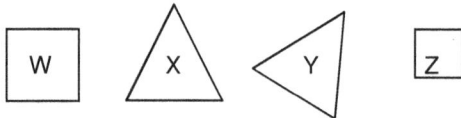

   A.   W and X   B. X and Y   C. W and Z

THURSDAY — Measurement

1. Liam biked 25 km in 1.5 hours. How long will it take for him to bike 100km?

2. Find the perimeter of an octagon with 3 cm sides.

3. What unit of measure would you use to measure the capacity of a juice carton?

4. Find the surface area of the figure.

   6 m   8 m   11 m

5. What is the area of the circle? Round to the nearest hundreth.
   Assume π = 3.14.

   m = 32 cm

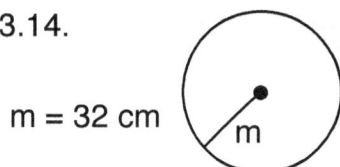

Data Management

The town of Melrose kept a record of its rainfall for six months. Here are the results:

Amount of Rainfall in Melrose

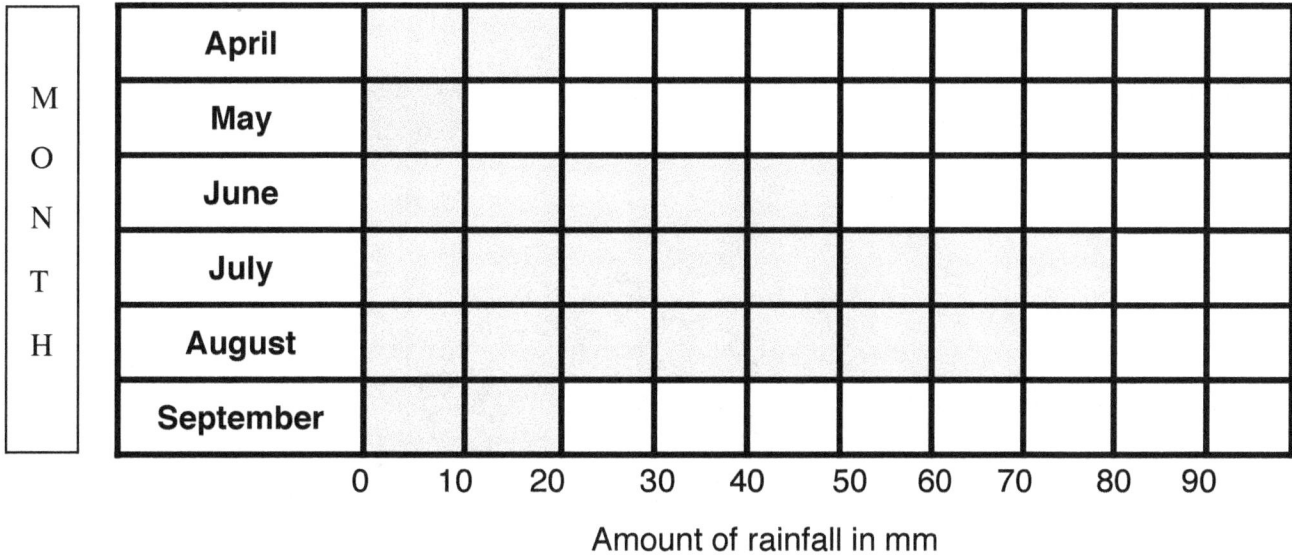

MONTH	0	10	20	30	40	50	60	70	80	90
April										
May										
June										
July										
August										
September										

Amount of rainfall in mm

1. Which months had more than 40 mm of rainfall? _____

2. Which month had the most rainfall? _____

3. How much rain fall was there altogether? _____

BRAIN STRETCH

Chris wanted to buy some soda pop for a party. He had a choice of buying a case of 24 cans of soda pop or 4 six-packs. One case of 24 soda pop cans costs $8.44. A six-pack of soda pop cans costs $2.95. Which is the better buy?

MONDAY Patterning and Algebra

1. What is the pattern rule?

   10, 23, 49, 101, 205

2. What kind of pattern is the pattern in question #1?

3. Fill in the missing number.

   1, 3, 7, 15, ____, 63

4. Complete by evaluating the expression.

   6*d*
   for *d* = 6

5. What is the missing number?

   11 X ____ = 176

TUESDAY Number Sense

1. Michael spent $1.55 on an ice cream cone and $0.95 on a soda. How much change will he get back from a five dollar bill?

2. Which of the following numbers is composite?

   4,   5,   9,   15

3. There are 20 cookies eaten out of a box of 40. What percent of the cookies has been eaten?

4. Write the following in decimal form.

   ten and nineteen hundredths

5. Multiply:

   56.41 X 1000 =

WEDNESDAY — Geometry

1. Classify the angle.

2. Is this an equilateral triangle?

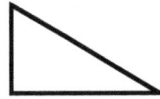

3. Which 3D figure has no faces?

    A. triangular prism
    B. sphere
    C. cone
    D. cylinder

4. Calculate the measure of the missing angle.

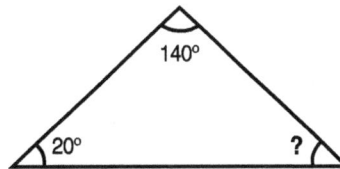

5. Are these shapes congruent or similar?

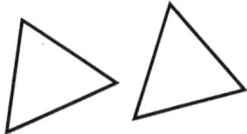

THURSDAY — Measurement

1. How are the area of a parallelogram and the area of a rectangle related?

2. 5.6 m = _____ dm

3. 3 years = ___ weeks?

4. Chris got home from baseball practice at 5:30 pm. What time is that in 24 hour notation?

5. What is the area? Round to the nearest hundredth. Assume $\pi = 3.14$.

m = 16

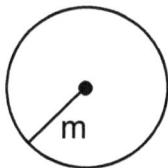

Sort factors into the Venn Diagram, using the rules listed below.

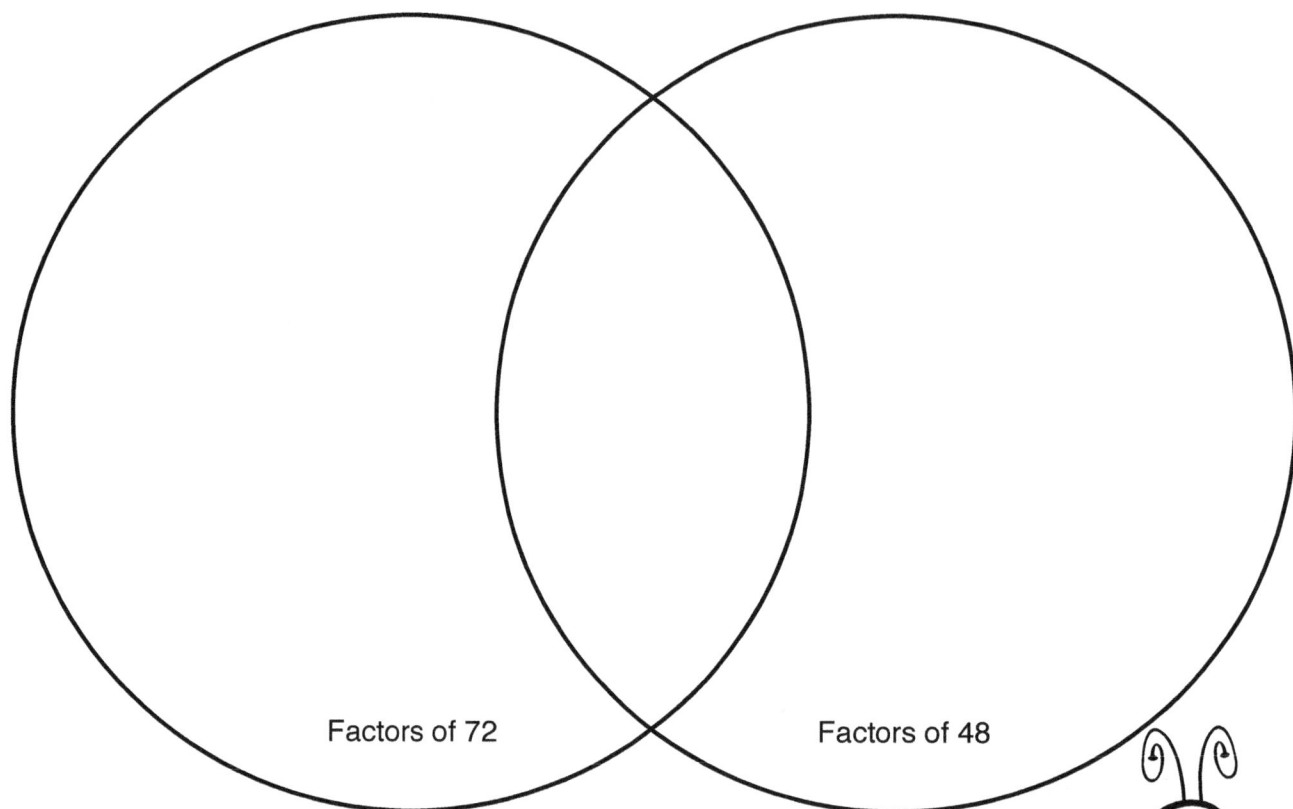

Factors of 72

Factors of 48

BRAIN STRETCH

A box of cookies weighs 420 grams. If Megan brought two boxes for the class party, what is the combined weight of both boxes of cookies in kilograms?

MONDAY — Patterning and Algebra

1. Complete the function table:

x	X + 25 - 5
1	
2	
3	
4	
5	

2. What are the first three numbers for this pattern rule?

   start at 880, subtract 25

3. Simplify the expression using the proper order of operations.

   $52 \div 4 + (63 \div 7 - 1)$

4. Fill in the missing number.

   5, 12, 26, _____, 110

5. Complete by evaluating the expression.

   $5g$
   for $g = 9$

TUESDAY — Number Sense

1. List the integers in order from least to greatest.

   -30, -24, 17, 47

2. Change the mixed number to an improper fraction.

   $3\frac{4}{7} =$

3. Divide:

   $3\overline{)93.6}$

4. In a class of 30, 18 students are girls. What is the ratio of girls to boys?

5. A bunch of flowers costs $8.99. How much will 5 bunches cost?

WEDNESDAY — Geometry

1. Look at the shapes. Name the transformation.

3. Are these shapes congruent or similar?

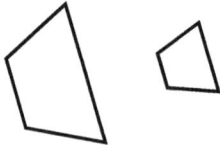

5. Which of these are parallelograms?

A. shapes B & A   B. shapes D& C   C. shapes B &D

3. How many lines of symmetry?

B

4. Which figure has more than 5 sides?

   A. trapezoid

   B. pentagon

   C. hexagon

THURSDAY — Measurement

1. What is the radius of a circle whose diameter is 64 cm?

2. How many decades in 6 centuries?

3. Find the area of this shape:

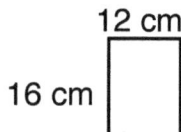

    12 cm

16 cm

4. 0.4 km = _____ dm

5. If the average speed of a motorist is 50 km per hour, calculate the distance if he or she travelled for 2 hours.

Data Management

Find the mean for each set of data on these stem and leaf plots.

1.

Stem	Leaves
15	1
16	1 2
17	4

2.

Stem	Leaves
1	3 5 6 7
2	3 8
3	0 0 2 6

BRAIN STRETCH

David ran 100 metres in 51 seconds. Paul ran 1 kilometre in 5 minutes 12 seconds. Who was the faster runner? Explain your thinking.

MONDAY — Patterning and Algebra

1. Complete by evaluating the expression.

   $8e + 5$
   for $e = 3$

2. Complete the function table.

x	2x +2
1	
2	
3	
4	
5	

3. What will be the 3rd number for this pattern rule?

   start at 4, multiply by 3

4. Create a repeating pattern.

5. Fill in the missing number.

   100, 300, 900, _____, 8100

TUESDAY — Number Sense

1. If you cut a cake into slices, choose which fraction shows the slice of cake that is the smallest piece.

   A. $\frac{1}{4}$ B. $\frac{1}{2}$ C. $\frac{3}{4}$

2. 8 is not a factor of:

   A. 48   B. 24   C. 52

3. Kaitlyn bought three notebooks at $2.35 each. How much did she spend in total?

4. Subtract:

   $25.6 - 12.07$

5. Write the following as a numeral.

   nine hundred eighteen thousand fifty-five

WEDNESDAY Geometry

1. How many vertices does a hexagonal prism have?

2. Are the shapes congruent or similar?

3. Classify this angle.

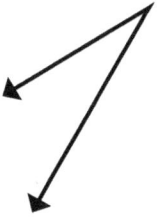

4. If the angles of a triangle measure 50°, 65° and 65°, what type of triangle is it?

5. How many edges does a cube have?

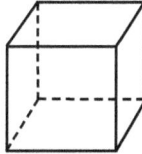

THURSDAY Measurement

1. What unit would you use to measure the mass of a vitamin tablet?

   A. mg   B. mm   C. ml

2. What time is 14:24 on a 12 hour clock?

3. What is the year 2 decades after 1969?

4. 0.5 km = _____ mm

4. If Mario drives 725 km to Montreal at a speed of 100 km per hour, how long will it take him to get there?

Data Management

Find the mean for each set of data.

1.

Stem	Leaves
33	1 2 7 8
34	1 5 5 5 6
17	4

2.

Stem	Leaves
11	7
12	1 5 8
13	0
14	
15	4 4 9

BRAIN STRETCH

Sophie made a round picture frame that is 20 cm in diameter. She wants to wrap a blue ribbon around the outside of the frame two times and needs to know how long the ribbon should be. How long should the ribbon be?

 Week 20

MONDAY — Patterning and Algebra

1. Fill in the missing number.

   1, 4, 9, 16, ___, 36

2. Complete by evaluating the expression.

   $9d + 4$
   for $d = 2$

3. Complete this function table:

x	36 - x
1	
2	
3	
4	
5	

4. Solve the equation.

   $42 \div n = 6$

5. What is the missing number?

   $144 \div$ _____ $= 12$

TUESDAY — Number Sense

1. Mr. Bruce gave out six prize pencils each week day. How many does he give away in nine weeks?

2. Divide: 60.5 by 5

3. Write 49 156 in words.

4. Jake's grandfather is 84 years old. What is his age in months?

5. Add:

   54 678 + 19 431 =

WEDNESDAY — Geometry

1. What 3D figure does this object look like?

   A. cone

   B. sphere

   C. cylinder

2. Classify the following group of lines:

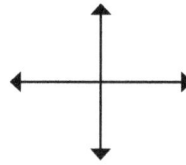

3. How many lines of symmetry?

   P

4. Which 3D figure has 8 edges?

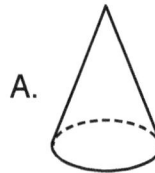 A. 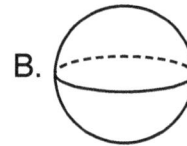 B. 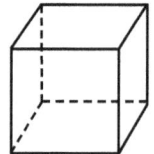 C.

   D. none

5. Which 3D figure has 12 edges?

THURSDAY — Measurement

1. Write the time difference.

   from 08:32 to 12:41

2. What tool would you use to measure the temperature?

3. How many centuries in 1200 years?

4. Calculate the volume.

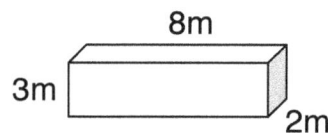

   8m

   3m

   2m

5. 650 mm = _____ cm

Mrs. Turnbull felt that a stop sign should be placed on the street in front of her house to stop cars from speeding down the road. She asked her daughter Madelyn to survey the number of cars that drove past their home every day for an hour after school. She created a pictograph to show her results.

Day	Number of Cars
Monday	🚗 🚗 🚗
Tuesday	🚗 🚗 🚗 🚗
Wednesday	🚗 🚗 🚗 🚗 🚗
Thursday	🚗 🚗 🚗 🚗
Friday	🚗 🚗 🚗

🚗 = 10 cars

1. What day did the most cars travel past Madelyn's house? _____

2. What day did the least number of cars pass her house?_____

3. How many cars did Madelyn count altogether?_____

4. What day did 50 cars pass her house? _____

5. What was the range number of cars that passed her house each day after school?_____

BRAIN STRETCH

Ross has twenty-one hammers in his toolbox. Two-thirds of them are broken. How many hammers are broken?

MONDAY — Patterning and Algebra

1. Simplify the expression using the proper order of operations.

   (89.52 + 3 + 24.33) - 5.7

2. Fill in the missing number.

   100, 121, 144, _____, 196

3. What is the missing number?

   180 X _____ = 0.18

4. What is the twentieth shape in this pattern?

5. Create a shrinking pattern.

TUESDAY — Number Sense

1. What is the value of 7 in the number 19 734?

   A.   70 000

   B.   7000

   C.   700

2. What is 1789 rounded to the nearest thousand?

3. Daniel buys 1:4 apples to oranges. If he bought 10 apples, how many oranges did he buy?

4. Choose: >, <, or =

   0.08 ☐ 1.08

5. What is the lowest common multiple of 2 and 10?

WEDNESDAY — Geometry

1. How many lines of symmetry does this number have?

   9

2. What are 4 sided figures called?

3. How many edges does rectangular prism have?

4. Classify this angle.

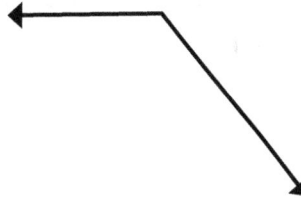

5. Name a quadrilateral that has two pairs of 90 degree angles?

THURSDAY — Measurement

1. 1.2 km = _____ dm

2. Write the time difference.

   from 08:45 to 16:20

3. What object is shorter in length than a decimetre?

   A. an ant   B. a bus   C. a metre stick

4. What year is 3 decades before 1969?

5. What is the best estimate for the mass of two books?

   A. 1 kg   B. 1 g   C. 1000 kg

Data Management

Mrs. Stephenson kept a gardener's journal to track the growth of her geranium plants. Here is the data she collected in July and August.

Plant	July	August
#1	10 cm	14 cm
#2	9 cm	11 cm
#3	12 cm	13 cm
#4	12 cm	15 cm
#5	11 cm	12 cm
#6	14 cm	17 cm
#7	8 cm	11 cm

1. What is the range of the data in July? _____

2. What is the mean height of the plants in July? _____

3. What is the range of the data in August? _____

4. What is the mean height of the plants in August? _____

5. What is the difference between the mean heights? _____

BRAIN STRETCH

Katherine has forty-two dresses. One-sixth of her dresses are blue. How many of Katherine's dresses are blue?

MONDAY — Patterning and Algebra

1. Fill in the missing number.

   50, 102, 206, ___, 830

2. Complete by evaluating the expression.

   $5d + 8$
   for $d = 3$

3. Which division fact has the same quotient as $48 \div 8$?

   A. $32 \div 4$ B. $48 \div 8$ C. $27 \div 3$

4. Solve the equation.

   $4 \times p = 56$

5. Create a repeating pattern using: ● ○

TUESDAY — Number Sense

1. Which even numbers are between 50 and 70 and are a multiple of six?

2. Divide:

   $19\overline{)76}$

3. Write the numeral in expanded form.

   569 831

4. How many of the following numbers are odd?

   15, 76, 23, 91, 40

   A. 3   B. 4   C. 5

4. Write as a decimal number.

   $\dfrac{40}{50}$

WEDNESDAY — Geometry

1. Calculate the measure of the missing angle.

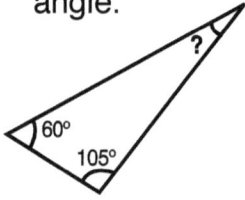

2. Name two 3D shapes that can roll.

3. Flip this shape over the line.

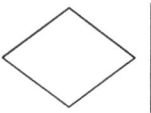

4. What shape is the face of a hexagonal prism?

5. Which 3D figure does this object look like?

THURSDAY — Measurement

1. What is the best estimate for the capacity of a cup of hot chocolate?

   A. 200 l   B. 200 ml   C. 2 ml

2. A rectangle is 9 cm long and 7cm wide. What is the perimeter if the length decreased by 2 cm?

3. 17.8 cm = _____m

4. Write the time difference.

   from 16:13 to 23:21

5. Calculate the area of the parallelogram.

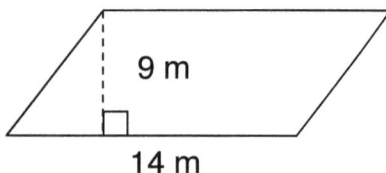

   9 m

   14 m

Data Management

Spencer had a bag of marbles. In his bag he had:

8 black marbles	18 red marbles
19 orange marbles	13 blue marbles

1. State the ratio of orange marbles to all the marbles.

2. State the ratio of blue marbles to all the marbles.

3. State the ratio of black marbles to orange and blue marbles.

4. State the ratio of red marbles to black marbles.

BRAIN STRETCH

If Baycrest Car Dealership sells 5 silver cars for every 2 red ones, how many silver cars did they sell last year if they sold 50 red cars?

MONDAY — Patterning and Algebra

1. Fill in the missing number.

   100, 125, 150, _____, 200

2. Complete by evaluating the expression.

   $6d - 4$
   for $d = 4$

3. Which multiplication fact has the same product as 8 X 5?

   A. 10 X 4   B. 7 X 6   C. 9 X 4

4. Solve the equation.

   $4 X p = 36$

5. Create a repeating pattern using numbers:

TUESDAY — Number Sense

1. Ben reads one comic book for every 5 novels. How many comics did Ben read if he read 20 novels?

2. Write the numeral 802 300 in words.

3. Subtract:

   775.25 – 30.12

4. What are the prime numbers between 30 and 35?

5. Write the decimal as a fraction.

   0.08

WEDNESDAY — Geometry

1. What makes two figures congruent?

2. What makes two figures similar?

3. What 3D figure does this object look like?

4. How many lines of symmetry?

G

5. How many of the following pairs of lines are parallel?

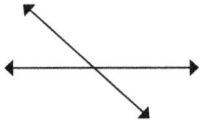

A. 1
B. 2
C. 3

THURSDAY — Measurement

1. If you are traveling 50 km per hour. How long would it take you to go 725 km?

2. 50 km = _____ cm

3. What is the area in square metres of a pool 16m X 18 m?

4. Find the perimeter of the octagon.

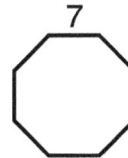

5. Calculate the area of the parallelogram.

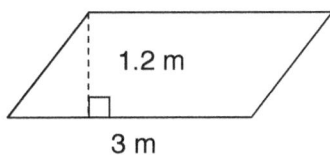

1.2 m

3 m

Here is a double bar graph of how much money two classes collected for a class trip.

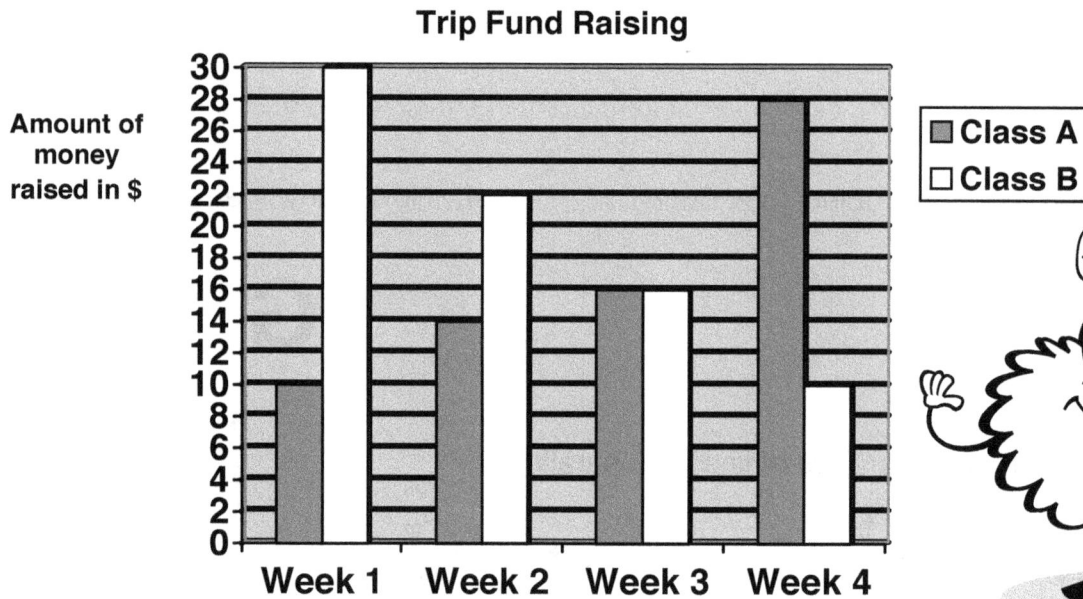

Trip Fund Raising

Amount of money raised in $

Legend:
- ■ Class A
- □ Class B

Week 1   Week 2   Week 3   Week 4

1. Which class raised the most money? _____

2. How much money did class A raise in weeks 3 and 4? _____

3. In what week did both classes raise the same amount of money? _____

4. How much money did class B raise in weeks 1 and 2? _____

BRAIN STRETCH

Two hundred sixty five people visited the circus on Tuesday, three hundred ninety-nine on Wednesday, and three hundred forty-one on Thursday. How many people visited the circus from Tuesday to Thursday?

MONDAY — Patterning and Algebra

1. What should replace the _____ to make the following equation true?

   8 X 3 = 99 _____ 75

   A. +   B. -   C. ÷

2. Create a repeating pattern.

3. What number comes next?

   774, 764, 754, _____

4. Complete the function table:

x	6x-1
1	
2	
3	
4	
5	

5. Indicate the value of b.

   $b \times 5 + 12 = 47$

TUESDAY — Number Sense

1. Write the improper fraction as a mixed number.

   $\dfrac{35}{2}$

2. Add:

   ```
     475
     591
   + 284
   ```

3. Write four hundred twenty-two dollars and nineteen cents in numerals.

4. Subtract:

   ```
     79 805
   - 35 752
   ```

5. What is the greatest common factor for 32 and 40?

WEDNESDAY   Geometry

1. Draw a pair of congruent figures.

2. How many lines of symmetry?

2. How many degrees are there in a circle?

4. What is an angle that is 45° called?

    A. right   B. acute C. straight D. obtuse

5. What 3D figure could be made from these pieces?

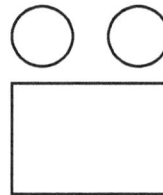

    A. cylinder   B. rectangular prism C. pyramid

THURSDAY   Measurement

1. How many minutes in 12 hours?

2. What is the area of this parallelogram?

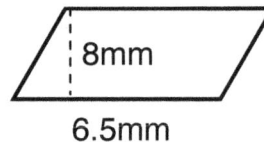

8mm

6.5mm

3. 6.50 km =_____cm

4. 36500 days = _____years

5. If you travel 78km in three hours, how fast are you traveling?

Donald's basketball team measured the height of each player and surveyed their shoe size to see if there was a relationship between the two measurements. Here are the results:

Player	Height	Shoe Size
Chris	190 cm	10
Mario	194 cm	10.5
Liam	180 cm	9
Deepak	182 cm	9.5
Steven	201 cm	11.5
Shawn	198 cm	11
Michael	202 cm	12
George	181 cm	10
Ben	175 cm	9
Spencer	180 cm	10
David	183 cm	10

1. What is the mean shoe size?_____

2. What is the mode shoe size?_____

3. What is the median shoe size?_____

4. What is the mean height of the players?_____

5. Is there a relationship between height and shoe size? Explain.

_____

BRAIN STRETCH

What is the better buy?

      A. 8 DVDs for $88   B. 21 DVDs for $168

MONDAY — Patterning and Algebra

1. What should replace the _____ to make the following equation true?

    $18 \div 3 = 42$ _____ 7

    A. +   B. -   C. ÷

2. Predict what the 16th animal will be in this pattern.

    A.   B.   C.

3. What number comes next?

    989, 979, 969, _____

4. Create a shrinking pattern.

5. Calculate the value of b.

    $b \times 5 - 10 = 90$

TUESDAY — Number Sense

1. What is 25% of 100

2. Multiply:

    $$\begin{array}{r} 987 \\ \times\ 34 \\ \hline \end{array}$$

3. What are the prime numbers between 15 and 25?

4. Multiply:

    59.41 X 1000

5. Simplify the expression using the order of operations.

    $(4 + 8) - (70 - 65)$

1. How are a triangle and a hexagon different?

2. How many lines of symmetry does this letter have?

V

3. Name the transformation. Choose reflection, translation or rotation

4. How many faces does a cylinder have?

5. Name the transformation. Choose reflection, translation or rotation.

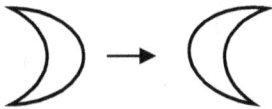

THURSDAY Measurement

1. What is the surface area of this prism?

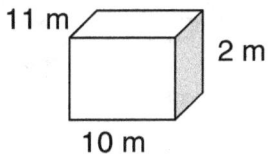

11 m

2 m

10 m

2. 0.02 l = _____ ml

3. 375.3 cm = _____ m

4. What is the volume of the shape in question 1?

5. Which shape has 2 pairs of parallel sides, and 2 pairs of angles that are equal?

A. △   B. ▱   C. ⏢

Complete the chart.

Set of Data	Mean	Range	Mode
1. 29, 29, 20, 4, and 28			
2. 13, 12, 6, 7, and 7			
3. 14, 17, 8, 14, and 2			
4. 7, 17, 17, 12, and 17			
5. 14, 18, 17, 18, and 18			

BRAIN STRETCH

What is a better buy?

    A.   11 pens for $2.64   B.   31 pens for $8.36

MONDAY — Patterning and Algebra

1. Find r.

   If $r - 6 = 22$.

2. Complete by evaluating the expression.

   $b^2 - 3b + 10$

   for $b = 12$

3. Complete the table:

x	2x + 3
1	
2	
3	
4	
5	

4. There are 12 roses in each vase. How many roses in 30 vases?

5. Create a growing pattern.

TUESDAY — Number Sense

1. Simplify the expression using the proper order of operations.

   $2 \times 3 - (12 - 8)$

2. Order this set from the least to the greatest part of a unit.

   $\frac{1}{4}$ 0.07   60 %

3. Divide:

   $4\overline{)688.4}$

4. What is 30% of $270.00?

5. What is the greatest common factor for 12 and 32?

WEDNESDAY Geometry

1. How many lines of symmetry does this number have?

3

2. Name a quadrilateral that has four equal sides.

3. Name one way the attributes of a rhombus and a trapezoid are the same.

4. What is the measure of the missing angle?

5. Are these shapes congruent or similar?

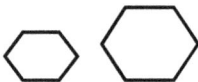

THURSDAY Measurement

1. If Bill can type 24 words per minute, how many can he type in an hour?

2. Find the surface area of the figure.

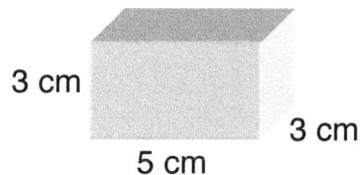

3 cm

3 cm

5 cm

3. Valerie got home from baseball practice at 9:30 pm. State the time in 24 hour notation.

4. A rectangle has an area of 84 cm^2. The width is 12 cm. What is the length?

5. How many days in 3 centuries?

Data Management

Mrs. Monroe took a survey of what foods her students preferred to buy from the cafeteria. Here are the results:

	Number of Votes
French Fries	18
Hamburgers	22
Meat Patties	11
Sandwiches	15
Salads	22
Soups	8

1. What was the most popular choice? _____

2. What was the least popular choice? _____

3. What is the range of the data collected? _____

4. What is the mean? _____

5. How many students were surveyed? _____

6. How many more students chose salads than French fries? _____

BRAIN STRETCH

At Big Bob's BBQ restaurant, rectangle tables were put together to sit people. A single rectangle table seats 4 people. Two rectangle tables placed together seats 8 people. How many people can be seated if 9 tables are placed together?

MONDAY — Patterning and Algebra

1. What should replace the _____ to make the following equation true?

   $9 \times 3 = 30$ _____ 3

   A. $+$ B. $-$ C. $\div$

2. Predict what the 16th animal will be in this pattern.

   A.
   B.
   C.

3. What number comes next?

   1000, 900, 800, _____

4. Create a repeating pattern.

5. Indicate the value of b.

   $b \times 6 + 3 = 39$

TUESDAY — Number Sense

1. Reduce the fraction to lowest terms.

   $\dfrac{16}{18}$

2. Find 75% of 32.

3. Write the decimal.

   two hundredths

4. Multiply and write the answer in simplest form:

   $7 \times \dfrac{2}{3}$

5. What are the prime numbers between 80 and 90?

Week 28

WEDNESDAY — Geometry

1. How are the attributes of a triangle and a hexagon different?

2. How many lines of symmetry does this letter have?

J

3. What is the measure of the missing angle?

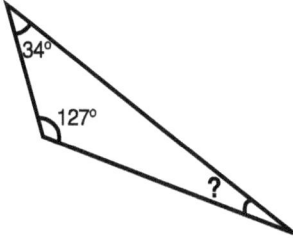

34°
127°
?

4. Name the transformation. Choose reflection, translation or rotation.

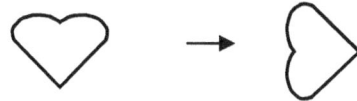

5. What is an angle of 53° called?

A. obtuse   B. right   C. acute

THURSDAY — Measurement

1. What is the best estimate for the length of a worm?

A. 3 cm   B. 3 m   C. 3 km

2. Craig lives 850 000 cm from his school. How many metres is that?

3. There are 20 g of candy in a bag. How many mg of candy are there in 2 bags?

4. It is now 12:36 pm. What time will it be in 38 minutes?7

5. A rectangle is 8 cm long and 6 cm wide. What is the perimeter if the length is decreased by 1 cm?

Data Management

Answer the probability questions using the information on the two spinners.

Spinner 1   **Spinner 2**

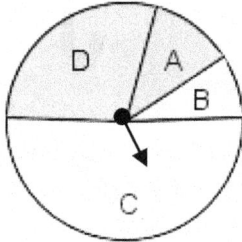   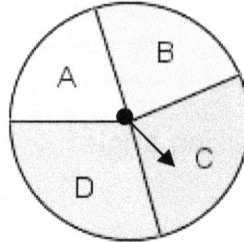

If someone has only 1 spin:

1. Is spinning C more probable on Spinner 1 or Spinner 2? _____

2. On which spinner is A more probable? _____

3. On which spinner is B less probable? _____

4. Which letter is equally likely on both Spinner 1 and Spinner 2? _____

BRAIN STRETCH

In how many ways can Stephen, Chris, and Mathew stand in line?

MONDAY — Patterning and Algebra

1. Ben has 30 bags of jelly beans. Each bag has 120 jelly beans. Which number sentence finds the total jelly beans Ben has?

   A. 30 x 120   B. 30 + 120   C. 120 ÷ 30

2. Predict what the 11th animal will be in this pattern.

   A.    B.   C.

3. What number comes next?

   725, 625, 525, _____

4. Complete by evaluating the expression.

   $b^2 - 3b + 10$

   for $b = 8$

5. Which number sentence has the same answer as 14 x 8?

   A. 120 – 8   B. 122 + 30   C. 100 ÷ 4

TUESDAY — Number Sense

1. Divide: 925.5 by 5

2. Write as a numeral:

   three hundred seventy-three thousand twelve

3. What is 10% of 30?

4. Order this set from the least to the greatest part of a unit.

   $\frac{1}{5}$ 70%   0.03

5. Which even number is between 40 and 50 and is a multiple of six?

   A. 42   B. 46   C. 44

WEDNESDAY — Geometry

1. What shape does this object look like?

STOP

2. How many lines of symmetry does this letter have?

G

3. Are these shapes congruent, similar or neither?

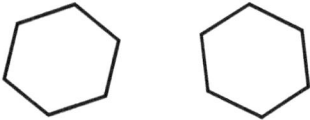

4. Name the transformation. Choose reflection, translation or rotation.

5. What is an angle of 140° called?

A. obtuse   B. right   C. acute

THURSDAY — Measurement

1. How many metres in 160 km?

2. 45 mg = _____ g

3. A rectangle has an area of 240 cm². The width is 15 cm. What is the length?

4. Each side of a pentagon measures 8 cm. What would the perimeter be if the sides were to increase by 2 cm each?

5. The time is 7:15 p.m. What time will it be in 2 hour and 10 minutes?

Banting Public School held their annual cookie sale. Here are the amounts of cookies sold.

Cookie	Cookies Sold
Oatmeal	198
Chocolate Chip	220
Double Chocolate	295
Vanilla Crème	165

1. List the types of cookies sold from least to greatest.

_____

2. What was the ratio of oatmeal cookies sold to vanilla crème? _____

3. How many more double chocolate cookies were sold than chocolate chip? _____

4. How many cookies were sold altogether? _____

5. If each cookie sold for $0.75, how much money was raised altogether? _____

BRAIN STRETCH

Katherine and Alexander went to the grocery store to buy 2 dozen eggs. When they opened the egg carton at home they saw that 1/4 of the eggs were broken.

1. How many eggs were broken?

2. How many eggs were not broken?

Patterning and Algebra

1. Simplify the expression using the proper order of operations.

   3 + 2 x 8 -1

2. Predict what the 15th animal will be in this pattern.

   A. 🐧   B. 🐨   C. 🐊

3. What number comes next?

   5, 25, 125, 625, _____

4. Complete by evaluating the expression.

   11 (9 + t) - 87

   for t = 43

5. Which number sentence has the same answer as 5 X 5?

   A. 120 − 8   B. 122 + 30   C. 100 ÷ 4

TUESDAY **Number Sense**

1. Which number comes between 4.57 and 4.74?

   A. 4.98   B. 4.63   C. 4.41

2. Which of the following numerals has a 6 in the hundredths place?

   A. 9.67   B. 6.79   C. 7.96

3. Write 6 ¾ as an improper fraction.

4. What is 25% of 200?

5. Which of the following numbers when rounded to the nearest 10 is 4230 and when rounded to the nearest 1000 is 4000?

   A. 4231   B. 3867   C. 4145

 Week 30

1. What 3D figure does this object look like?

2. How many lines of symmetry does this letter have?

C

3. Are these shapes congruent, similar or neither?

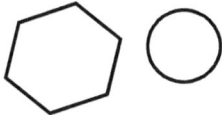

4. Name the transformation. Choose reflection, translation or rotation.

5. What is an angle of 34° called?

    A. obtuse   B. right   C. acute

THURSDAY   Measurement

1. 26 900 cg = _____ kg

2. David could shoot 18 baskets in one minute. How many should he be able to shoot in an hour?

3. Find the surface area of the figure.

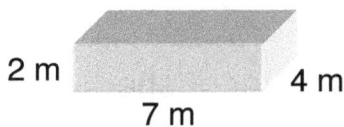

2 m   4 m
    7 m

4. An aquarium is 12 m wide, 18 m long and 5 m deep. What is its volume?

5. Calculate the perimeter.

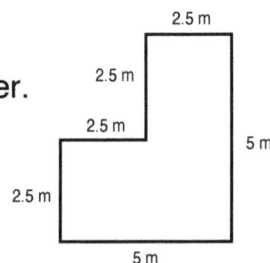

2.5 m

2.5 m

2.5 m

5 m

2.5 m

5 m

Use the information below to complete the questions.

A																				
B																				
C																				
D																				
E																				

There are 20 spaces in each row:

1. Which row shows 50% of the row is filled? _____

2. Which row shows 0.25 of the row is filled? _____

3. What percent of row B is filled? _____

4. How much more of row A is filled than row D? _____

5. Which row is filled between ¼ and ½? _____

BRAIN STRETCH

When Sophie has something to drink, 2 out of 5 times it is water. If she has 50 drinks in a week, how many of them will be water?

Math — Show What You Know!

_____

☐ I read the question and I know what I need to find.

☐ I drew a picture or a diagram to help solve the question.

☐ I showed all the steps in solving the question.

☐ I used math language to explain my thinking.

Student Tracking Sheet

Student	Week 1	Week 2	Week 3	Week 4	Week 5	Week 6	Week 7	Week 8	Week 9	Week 10	Week 11	Week 12	Week 13	Week 14	Week 15

Student Tracking Sheet

Student	Week 16	Week 17	Week 18	Week 19	Week 20	Week 21	Week 22	Week 23	Week 24	Week 25	Week 26	Week 27	Week 28	Week 29	Week 30

You Are Incredible!

Keep Up the Good Work!

_____

Week 1

Mon.   **1.** 32 **2.** 9 **3.** start at 2, multiply by 2 add 1 **4.** 295 **5.** 3, 6, 12

Tues.   **1.** 275 **2.** 28 229, 28 989, 28 999 **3.** 12.5
   4. two hundred thirty-four thousand three hundred forty **5.** $7.25

Wed.   **1.** ans. can vary ▭ ▫ ▱ **2.** right **3.** ⇐ **4.** 2 **5.** acute

Thurs.   **1.** 300 000 **2.** 0.0007km **3.** b **4.** 56m² **5.** 6.8m

Fri.   **1.** 42 **2.** Panthers **3. 49** **4.** 50 **5. bar graph**

Brain Stretch   1. c 2. c 3. c 4. p 5. c 6.c

Week 2

Mon.   **1.** 3, 30, 300 **2.** 111 **3.** 425 **4.** ans.will vary **5.** ◇

Tues.   **1.** 9129, 9291, 19 912 **2.** eight hundred seventy-six dollars and ninety cents
   3. < **4.** 1/8, 4/8, 5/8, 7/8 **5.** 81

Wed.   **1.** 5 **2.** b **3.** rhombus **4.** 8 **5.** an angle more than 90° and less than 180°

Thurs.   **1.** September **2.** baking a cake **3.** 5000ml **4.** 13 **5.** <

Fri.   **1.** 20 **2.** 36 **3.** 129, 142 **4.** Cameron, 162 cm

Brain Stretch $90

Week 3

Mon.   **1.** 10 **2.** 101 **3.** 55, 44 **4.** 3, 15, 75 **5.** 3

Tues.   **1.** $1.29 **2.** 6/10 or 3/5 **3.** 342 **4.** 1110 1101, 1011, 1001, **5.** 1300

Wed.   **1.** trapezoid **2.** 1 **3.** congruent **4.** 4 **5.** an angle less than 90°

Thurs.   **1.** 10 months **2.** 69m **3.** 4cm² **4.** 730 **5.** b

Fri.   **1.** comedy **2.** drama **3.** 10 **4.** 70 **5.** ans. will vary

Brain Stretch **1.** thousands **2.** tens **3.** ten thousands **4.** ones **5.** ten thousands **6.** hundred thousands

Week 4

Mon.   **1.** 488, 484, 480 **2.** 30, 38, 46 **3.** start at 3, multiply by 4 **4.** 14 **5.** 9/24

Tues.   **1.** 5600 **2.** 1, 2, 7, 14 **3.** 1127 **4.** $10 bill, 2 x toonies, 3 x quarters, 2 x dimes, 3 x pennies **5.** =

Wed.   **1.** c **2.** a **3.** rectangular prism **4.** parallelogram/ rhombus **5.** 4 sided polygon

Thurs.   **1.** 0.89cl **2.** 11:04pm **3.** garbage can **4.** 34 **5.** >

Fri.   **1.** 6 **2.** 1, 2, 3, 4, 5, 6 **3.** 1/2 **4.** 1/2 **5.** 1/6

Brain Stretch   8 squares

Week 5

Mon.   **1.** ans.will vary **2.** 3 **3.** start at 37, subtract 4 **4.** 22, 27 **5.** c

Tues.   **1.** 3/4 **2.** 702, 782, 827, 872 **3.** a **4.** 9471 **5.** seventy-seven dollars and thirty-five cents

Wed.   **1.** cylinder **2.** circle **3.** 3 **4.** b **5.** 5

Thurs.   **1.** a **2.** 9.6mm **3.** 312 weeks **4.** a **5.** 12 000

Fri. ans. will vary **1.** likely **2.** likely **3.** certain **4.** likely **5.** likely **6.** certain

Brain Stretch   1. 2385 2. 4536 3. 19.52 4. 8.14 5. 71.40

Week 6

Mon. **1.** 88 **2.** ans. will vary **3.** 96, 192 **4.** 2 **5.** start at 50, subtract 1, then subtract one more each time

Tues. **1.** 1, 2, 4, 5, 8, 10, 20, 40 **2.** 1xfifty, 2xdimes, 3xpennies **3.** 2/9, 5/9, 7/9 **4.** 6.931 **5.** eight thousand nine hundred fifty-four

Wed. **1.** 1 **2.** yes **3.** cube **4.** acute **5.** 8

Thurs. **1.** a **2.** 1988 **3.** 26m **4.** 220mm **5.** b

Fri. **1.** b **2.** f **3.** i **4.** d **5.** j **6.** h **7.** c **8.** a **9.** e **10.** g

Brain Stretch **1.** 100 000 + 30 000 + 2000 + 500 + 40 + 7 **2.** 30 000 + 3000 + 600 + 50 + 1
3. 90 000 + 4000 + 800 + 30 **4.** 100 000 + 90 000 + 1000 + 200 + 30 + 4

Week 7

Mon. **1.** 127 **2.** start at 1, add 10 **3.** 947 **4.** 72, 80, 88 **5.** 354

Tues. **1.** 655 012 **2.** 1233 **3.** 1980 **4.** 564 **5.** 2 pieces

Wed. **1.** sphere **2.** 5 **3.** a **4.** 4 **5.** b

Thurs. **1.** 7:30, 10.5hrs per week **2.** 63m **3.** 10521.067g **4.** 3720 **5.** 6.82 kg

Fri. **1.** 310 **2.** 190 **3.** 120 **4.** bar graph **5.** 6

Brain Stretch **1.** 156 hours **2.** 1560 hours

Week 8

Mon. **1.** 60 **2.** b **3.** 112 **4.** 23, 36, 62 **5.** start at 500, divide by 10

Tues. **1.** $776.51 **2.** hundreds **3.** 5.7 **4.** 400 000 + 80 000 + 2 000 + 900 + 30 + 7 **5.** 18

Wed. **1.** cone **2.** a **3.** an angle greater than 90° and less than 180° **4.** 40 degrees **5.** 0

Thurs. **1.** 56m **2.** a **3.** 0.559m **4.** kg **5.** 256 mins

Fri. **1.** approx. 16 **2.** 21/100 or 18.9/90 **3.** 52/100 or 46.8/90 **4.** 39% **5.** Bus

Brain Stretch **1.** 400km **2.** 800km

Week 9

Mon. **1.** 145, 289, 577 **2.** start at 1, x5-1 **3.** 454, 444, 434 **4.** 27 **5.** growing

Tues. **1.** > **2.** $80.88 **3.** one hundred twenty-eight thousand four hundred **4.** c **5.** 56

Wed. **1.** 4 sided polygon **2.** 60^0 **3.** **4.** rectangular prism **5.** c

Thurs. **1.** 84 **2.** 370ml **3.** 28m^2 **4.** 0.37km **5.** m

Fri. **1.** 148 **2.** Kaitlyn **3.** Madelyn and Michael/ Spencer and Megan **4.** 48 **5.** 8

Brain Stretch 2 is the better buy because each book is $9

Week 10

Mon. **1.** start at 78, add 7 to the column to the left **2.** 62 **3.** 30 000 000 **4.** 20, 43, 89 **5.** 111

Tues. **1.** 70 + 7 + 0.01 **2.** 7.996 **3.** 3/4 **4.** 149 141 **5.** 17/5

Wed. **1.** **2.** 1 **3.** 120^0 **4.** 2 **5.** 6

Thurs. **1.** mm or cm **2.** 9m x 9m **3.** 1000 years **4.** 3:20:15 **5.** 18 m

Fri. **1.** approx. 7 **2.** ¼ or 25/100 **3.** 45/100 or 36/80 **4.** 30% **5.** summer

Brain Stretch **1.** 0.227 **2.** 0.014 **3.** 8.65 **4.** 3.71 **5.** 5.722 **6.** 8.412

Week 11

Mon.   **1.** 12 **2.** 10, 15, 30 **3.** b **4.** shrinking **5.** 45, 36, 27

Tues.   **1.** 41.279 **2.** 5 3/4 **3.** 45 789.6 **4.** b **5.** 25 330

Wed.   **1.** triangle **2.** acute **3.** 1 **4.** 180^0 **5.** 1 or 0 – ans. may vary - discuss

Thurs. **1.** 299mm **2.** $18.9m^2$ **3.** kg **4.** 4 **5.** 9cm

Fri.   **1.** 93 **2.** 15 **3.** 13 **4.** 16.8 or rounded to 17

Brain Stretch   1. 25/30 or 5/6   2. 16.6%

Week 12

Mon.   **1.** 0.009 **2.** 100 **3.** 190, 175, 160 **4.** a **5.** 200km

Tues.   **1.** 240 **2.** 5/6 **3.** 98 521 **4.** 0.3 **5.** 100

Wed.   **1.** 60^0 **2.** a **3.** c **4.** 0 **5.** 8

Thurs. **1.** 12:57 pm **2.** 40 **3.** 38 **4.** 24 cm^2 **5.** 73 100

Fri.   1. 16.2, 9, 18, 20 **2.** 13, 16, 16.5, 17 **3.** 20.6, 5, 21, 21 **4.** 4, 3, 5, 5 **5.** 13, 15, 10, 10

Brain Stretch   154

Week 13

Mon.   **1.** square **2.** repeating **3.** 1422 **4.** 10, 20, 40 **5.** 10

Tues.   **1.** 9/100 **2.** 0.54 **3.** 276.0 **4.** 79.375 **5.** 375

Wed.   **1.** isosceles **2.** 0 **3.** $24cm^3$ **4.** 8 **5.** slide

Thurs. **1.** 185 cm **2.** 3cm **3.** 44cm **4.** 3pm **5.** 60

Fri.   **1.** 90 **2.** football, basketball, baseball, hockey **3.** 55 **4.** hockey **5.** football

Brain Stretch   193 boxes

Week 14

Mon.   **1.** 22 **2.** 3 **3.** 55 **4.** start at 5, add 3 **5.** 90, 86, 82

Tues.   **1.** 42 **2.** 0.01, 0.11, 1.01, 1.10 **3.** 87 481 **4.** 123 904 **5.** 12

Wed.   **1.** right **2.** 0 **3.** cube **4.** 60 m^2 **5.** 4

Thurs. **1.** 6000 **2.** 8:00pm **3.** $280m^2$ **4.** 4:30 **5.** 25cm

Fri.   factors for 45: 1, 3, 5, 9, 15, 45 factors for 36: 1, 2, 3, 4, 6, 9, 12, 18, 36 both: 1,3, 9,

Brain Stretch   **1.** $2.40 **2.** 2

Week 15

Mon.   **1.** 8 **2.** 8, 16, 24, 32, 40   **3.** start at 30, add 30 **4.** 384 **5.** face

Tues.   **1.** 101.23 **2.** a **3.** 24 **4.** 20 **5.** 216

Wed.   **1.** sphere **2.** 2 **3.** c **4.** 60^0 **5.** parallel

Thurs. **1.** km **2.** 36 000 **3.** 1/2bxh **4.** 8cm **5.** 225km

Fri.   **1.** 18 **2.** 10 **3.** chocolate **4.** bubble gum

Brain Stretch $67.50, No, because that is not enough.

Week 21

Mon. **1.** 25 **2.** 22 **3.** 35, 34, 33, 32, 31 **4.** 7 **5.** 12

Tues. **1.** 270 **2.** 12.1 **3.** forty-nine thousand one hundred fifty-six **4.** 1008 **5.** 74109

Wed. **1.** a **2.** 2 intersecting **3.** 0 **4.** d. none **5.** rectangular prism

Thurs. **1.** 4:09 **2.** thermometer **3.** 12 **4.** 48m^3 **5.** 65cm

Fri. **1.** Wednesday **2.** Monday, Friday **3.** 190 cars **4.** Wednesday **5.** 20

Brain Stretch   14

Week 22

Mon. **1.** 111.15 **2.** 169 **3.** 0.001 **4.** white heart **5.** ans will vary

Tues. **1.** c **2.** 2000 **3.** 40 **4.** < **5.** 10

Wed. **1.** 0 **2.** quadrilaterals **3.** 12 **4.** obtuse **5.** rectangle or square

Thurs. **1.** 12000dm **2.** 7:35 **3.** a **4.** 1939 **5.** a

Fri. **1.** 6 **2.** 11 cm **3.** 6 **4.** 13 **5.** 2cm

Brain Stretch   7

Week 23

Mon. **1.** 414 **2.** 23 **3.** b **4.** 14 **5.** ans will vary

Tues. **1.** 54,60,66 **2.** 4 **3.** 500 000+60 000+9000+800+30+1 **4.** a **5.** 0.8

Wed. **1.** 15^0 **2.** ans. will vary (sphere, cylinder, cone) **3.** see flip **4.** hexagon, rectangle or square
   5. rectangular prism

Thurs. **1.** b **2.** 28cm **3.** 0.178 **4.** 7:08 **5.** 126 m^2

Fri. **1.** 19:58 **2.** 13:58 **3.** 8:32 **4.** 18:8

Brain Stretch   125

Week 24

Mon. **1.** 175 **2.** 20 **3.** a **4.** 9 **5.** ans will vary

Tues. **1.** 4 **2.** eight hundred two thousand three hundred **3.** 745.13 **4.** 31 **5.** 8/100, 2/25

Wed. **1.** same size and shape **2.** same shape **3.** cube **4.** 0 **5.** b

Thurs. **1.** 14 hours 30 minutes **2.** 5 000 000cm **3.** 288m^2 **4.** 56 **5.** 3.6 m^2

Fri. **1.** class b **2.** $44 **3.** week 3 **4.** $52

Brain Stretch   1005 people

Week 25

Mon. **1.** b **2.** ans will vary **3.** 744 **4.** 5, 11, 17, 23, 29 **5.** 7

Tues. **1.** 17 1/2 **2.** 1350 **3.** $422.19 **4.** 44 053 **5.** 8

Wed. **1.** see drawing **2.** 1 **3.** 360^0 **4.** b **5.** a

Thurs. **1.** 720 **2.** 52mm^2 **3.** 650 000cm **4.** 100 **5.** 26km/hr

Fri. **1.** 10 **2.** 10 **3.** 10 **4.** 188 **5.** yes

Brain Stretch   b is $8 each

Week 26

Mon.   **1.** c **2.** b **3.** 959 **4.** ans. will vary **5.** 20

Tues.   **1.** 25 **2.** 33 558 **3.** .17, 19, 23 **4.** 59410 **5.** 7

Wed.   **1.** hexagon has 6 sides and triangle has three sides **2.** 1 **3.** translation **4.** 2 **5.** flip or reflection

Thurs.   **1.** $304m^2$ **2.** 20ml **3.** 3.753m **4.** $220m^3$ **5.** b

Fri.   **1.** 22, 25, 29 **2.** 9, 7, 7 **3.** 11, 15, 14 **4.** 14, 10, 17 **5.** 17, 4, 18

Brain Stretch   **1.** a

Week 27

Mon.   **1.** 28 **2.** 118 **3.** 5, 7, 9, 11, 13 **4.** 360 **5.** ans will vary

Tues.   **1.** 2 **2.** 0.07, ¼, 60% **3.** 172.1 **4.** $81.00 **5.** 4

Wed.   **1.** 1 **2.** square **3.** ans will vary (ie. Four sides) **4.** 65^0 **5.** similar

Thurs.   **1.** 1440 **2.** $78cm^2$ **3.** 21:30 **4.** 7cm **5.** 109500 days

Fri.   1. hamburgers and salads 2. soups 3. 14 4. 16 5. 96 6. 4

Brain Stretch   36

Week 28

Mon.   **1.** b **2.** b **3.** 700 **4.** ans will vary **5.** 6

Tues.   **1.** 8/9 **2.** 24 **3.** 0.02 **4.** 14/3 or 4 2/3 **5.** 83, 89

Wed.   **1.** ans will vary (ie. Number of sides, interior angles) **2.** 0 **3.** 19^0 **4.** rotation **5.** c

Thurs.   **1.** a **2.** 8500m **3.** 40000mg **4.** 1:14p.m. **5.** 26cm

Fri.   **1.** spinner 1 **2.** spinner 2 **3.** spinner 1 **4.** D

Brain Stretch   6

Week 29

Mon.   **1.** a **2.** b **3.** 425 **4.** 50 **5.** a

Tues.   **1.** 185.1 **2.** 373 012 **3.** 3 **4.** 0.03, 1/5, 70% **5.** a

Wed.   **1.** octagon **2.** 0 **3.** congruent **4.** rotation **5.** a

Thurs.   **1.** 160 000m **2.** 0.045g **3.** 16cm **4.** 50cm **5.** 9:25p.m.

Fri.   **1.** vanilla crème, oatmeal, chocolate chip, double chocolate **2.** 198:165 **3.** 75 **4.** 878 **5.** $658.50

Brain Stretch   **1.** 6 **2.** 18 eggs

Week 30

Mon.   **1.** 18 **2.** b **3.** 3125 **4.** 485 **5.** c

Tues.   **1.** b **2.** c **3.** 27/4 **4.** 50 **5.** a

Wed. **1.** cube **2.** 1 **3.** neither **4.** translation **5.** c

Thurs.   **1.** 2.69kg **2.** 1080 **3.** $100m^2$ **4.** $1080m^3$ **5.** 20m

Fri.   **1.** e **2.** d **3.** 70% **4.** 14 spaces or 70% **5.** c

Brain Stretch   20

Week 16

Mon.   **1.** 411, 415, 419 **2.** 12 **3.** ⤵ **4.** 120 legs **5.** 5

Tues.   **1.** 11,13, 17,19 **2.** 490.119 **3.** 0.0012 **4.** 202 **5.** -11, -10, -6, 9, 14, 15

Wed.   **1.** both are quadrilaterals, have parallel lines & right angles **2.** 4 **3.** 1 pair **4.** right **5.** 30^0

Thurs.   **1.** 4 **2.** ml **3.** 20:00 **4.** 10:33 am **5.** 72m

Fri.   **1.** blue **2.** orange, red, purple **3.** blue **4.** orange, red, purple

Brain Stretch $9.65

Week 17

Mon.   **1.** 19.7 **2.** 5.1, 5.22, 5.5, 5.6 **3.** 2.5116 **4.** 15, 16, 17, 18, 19 **5.** 844

Tues.   **1.** 60 **2.** 879 **3.** $2574 **4.** 12459 **5.** b

Wed.   **1.** 5 **2.** a **3.** an angle greater than 90° **4.** 180^0 **5.** b

Thurs.   **1.** 6 hours **2.** 24cm **3.** ml or L **4.** $404m^2$ **5.** $3215.36m^2$

Fri.   **1.** June, July and August **2.** July **3.** 250mm

Brain Stretch   Case of 24 is the best buy

Week 18

Mon.   **1.** start at 10, x2+3 **2.** growing **3.** 31 **4.** 36 **5.** 16

Tues.   **1.** $2.50 **2.** 4, 9, 15 **3.** 50% **4.** 10.19 **5.** 56 410

Wed.   **1.** straight **2.** no **3.** b **4.** 20^0 **5.** congruent

Thurs.   **1.** both lxw or lxh, same **2.** 56 **3.** 156 **4.** 17:30 **5.** $803.84m^2$

Fri.   **1.** Factors for 72: 1, 2, 3, 4, 6, 8, 9, 12, 18, 24, 36, 72 Factors for 48: 1, 2, 3, 4, 6, 8, 12, 16, 24, 48
        Both: 1, 2, 3, 4, 6, 8, 12, 24

Brain Stretch   0.84kg

Week 19

Mon.   **1.** 21, 22, 23, 24, 25 **2.** 880, 855, 830 **3.** 21 **4.** 54 **5.** 45

Tues.   **1.** -30, -24, 17, 47 **2.** 25/7 **3.** 31.2 **4.** 18:12 **5.** $44.95

Wed.   **1.** turn **2.** 1 **3.** similar **4.** c **5.** a

Thurs.   **1.** 32cm **2.** 60 **3.** $192cm^2$ **4.** 4600dm **5.** 100km

Fri.   A. 162 B. 24

Brain Stretch   Paul

Week 20

Mon.   **1.** 29 **2.** 4, 6, 8, 10, 12 **3.** 36 **4.** ans will vary **5.** 2700

Tues.   **1.** a **2.** c **3.** $7.05 **4.** 13.53 **5.** 918 055

Wed.   **1.** 12 **2.** congruent **3.** acute angle **4.** isosceles **5.** 12

Thurs.   **1.** a **2.** 2:24 pm **3.** 1989 **4.** 500 000mm **5.** 7.25 hours

Fri.   **1.** mean=340 **2.** mean=136

Brain Stretch 125.6 cm